LEGENDS
IN THE
GARDEN

LEGENDS
IN THE
GARDEN

WHO IN THE WORLD IS
NELLIE STEVENS?

LINDA L. COPELAND AND ALLAN M. ARMITAGE

FOREWORD BY RICHARD W. LIGHTY, PH.D.

WINGS
PUBLISHERS

Published by
Wings Publishers
1700 Chattahoochee Avenue
Atlanta, Georgia 30318

Book design and composition by Melanie M. McMahon

Manufactured in the United States of America

10 9 8 7 6 5 4
First Edition

ISBN 1-930897-08-1

CONTENTS

FOREWORD

In my garden are plants given to me by friends, neighbors and relatives; and plants filched, usually with permission, as seed or cuttings from far-off places or places special to me for historical, personal or botanical reasons. As I weed among them, walk by with Sally or ride by on the mower, these plants constantly send pleasant messages to me about these connections with people and times past. This is a big part of the intellectual delight of the garden.

Who among us gardeners has not puzzled over the obscure name of a plant of which we are fond, or delighted in the knowledge of a plant's connections with great people, renowned institutions or far-away places? If you are one of these then welcome to a feast of interesting, enjoyable and romantic anecdotes, and open further the doors to that intellectual garden where our lives become entwined with the men and women who first recognized the special virtues of our garden plants.

The commemoration of people and places through the naming of plants is as old as gardening itself. It celebrates the very human activities that have given us many of our best garden plants. From ancient common names Like Queen Anne's lace to formal honorific designations of the 19th Century like *Syringa* 'Andenken An Ludwig Spaeth' and the appellations of modern cultivars such as those discussed in this book, names are the key, but only the key, to the fascinating story of the origin of garden plants. They unlock the dimension beyond the art and science of cultivation, the dimension of intellectual satisfaction and delight in making connections. This is the province of this book: the stories behind the plants we grow. It makes for good conversation and good memories.

It is obviously impossible to catalogue the thousands of stories connected with even one good garden—the stories of each of the daffodils, daylilies, rhododendrons, iris and marigolds. It is possible, as this book clearly and in a delightful manner shows, to capture the spirit of the process of finding, recognizing, naming and introducing special plants, and to get a glimpse of the interconnections among gardeners and plantsmen which is a part of that process.

However you came to pick this book up, if what you have read so far entices you to go on, I assure you that your journey will be a pleasant one.

Richard W. Lighty, Ph.D.
Springwood
Kennett Square, PA
2001

ACKNOWLEDGMENTS

Many thanks for the tremendous support of our families and friends; without their encouragement this book would not have been written.

Marian Gordin's editing was much appreciated; the book is far better because of her efforts.

Within the book countless people are mentioned whose generous assistance was invaluable; many thanks, many times over.

We are indebted to Dr. Richard Lighty for his belief in the work, and his thoughtful foreword for the book.

PREFACE

Allan Armitage had the idea this book should be written. Convinced plantlovers everywhere would enjoy the stories behind the cultivar names of American garden plants, he challenged me to uncover them. I decided to go to work when Allan agreed to join in the writing; immediately, I became consumed in my pursuit. Recording the stories has been a rewarding experience and I shall be forever grateful to him for presenting me the opportunity to explore.

Plant and garden enthusiasts regularly encounter plants with names of people and places; however, many times the meaning of these names remains a mystery. To reveal these accounts is the purpose of this book. The people who are involved, although from many different backgrounds, inspire us with their utmost dedication to their passion for plants and provide insight into the various paths taken in order to contribute to the American plant palette. The plants which they have named to honor others, or those named to honor them or the places significant to them, have become our *Legends in the Garden*.

Because we feel too little of American garden history has been told, we based our selection on American garden plants only. The ones we have chosen are some familiar to us, suggested to us, and believed by us to have historical value in American horticulture. We acknowledge our list is by no means complete and apologize for the ones we neglected.

The research was accomplished in numerous ways. Many plant names are recent and sufficiently familiar to require only the simple task of contacting the growers, nursery people, gardeners, or family and friends about the plant's history. But, many of the portfolios required more time and energy and I depended greatly on recent technological innovations such as email and faxes, especially for immediate contact and quick information. A number of times the internet helped me locate a person's address and phone number, or find books no longer in print. It also served as a great tool for gathering additional information about the plants and people.

Talking with the people was the ultimate adventure and reward. Hundreds obliged my requests for interviews, information and photographs. Many times they were directly involved with naming the plants, but unfortunately, far too often the subjects of the stories are deceased, and, on more than one occasion, the person died during the time the research was conducted. In these cases, recording the stories became even more meaningful. For some of the narratives I traveled to meet with the subjects or their families; always, the meeting was most pleasant. Those individuals who contributed information are recognized at the conclusion of each story, and to all I express my endless appreciation for their patience and willingness to help.

And, we are thankful for the photographs received from many sources. A picture of the legendary person or place framed by the garden marker appears on the opening page of each story. Color photographs of the plants are contained in a separate section of the book. The pictures add immensely to our accounts.

During the four years of work since Allan originally suggested the project, I have collected many of the plants from our stories for my own garden. Each time I come upon one of these legends in my garden, I am reminded of its history. Knowing these stories has provided even greater pleasure to my garden visits. I hope the same will be true for all who read them. Recording them has been a privilege.

Linda L. Copeland
October, 2001

INTRODUCTION

Thought of this author:

Life is short, as the pundits say. Blink and we are gone. If we are lucky, we enjoy life, if we are very lucky, we leave behind children who will remember us fondly, and if we are exceedingly lucky, we will leave behind a legacy. Legacies take on many forms, but in the world of gardening, there are few more worthy legacies than being associated with a respected garden plant. This book is about those people and places who have left their names on some of our most cherished plants. It is unabashedly enthusiastic about the plants and the names associated with them. It is a history book, something sadly lacking in American horticulture, but is more of a celebration of the people and places, and a thank you for the plants which bear their names. Many of those people are no longer alive, some are elderly and others have miles to go before they even get tired. However, it has been fun to share their stories so that they will always remain an important part of American horticulture.

How we chose the stories:

There are many names associated with American garden plants, but we decided to concentrate only on people or places associated with a variety or cultivar of a plant. Thus we included Nellie Stevens and her holly and Frances Williams and her hosta but did not include William Bartram and David Fairchild whose names are indelibly associated with plant exploration and American horticulture. Sufficient literature already exists on these incredible people, yet how much do we know about Loie Benedict, other than her pulmonaria or Betty Corning, other than her clematis. We selected people and places associated with relatively well-known plants, and shied away from little known cultivars, although we admit to being somewhat subjective in our selections. This is no way diminishes the value of plants not chosen but we had to draw the line somewhere. By only including cultivars bearing the name of an individual or a place, we left out many very popular plants bred by or found by individuals, but with descriptive, rather than personal, names. And without doubt, we neglected a few plants we should have included. With apologies in advance, perhaps the next time around.

In reading through the stories, it is plain that a number of influential people do not have a chapter by their name. However, it would be inexcusable not to note the horticultural contribution of people like J.C. McDaniel, Michael Dirr, Allen Bush, Jerry Flintoff, Roger Gossler and countless others who noticed the horticultural value of many of these plants and encouraged their introduction.

How plants came to bear the cultivar name:

Our stories deal with cultivar names, which, to the average reader, may be a puzzling term. The term cultivar is associated with a variety of a plant with slightly different characteristics than another. For example, think of the hundreds of azaleas for sale in the shop each spring, they all are essentially the same plant but differ perhaps in flower color, flower size or habit. Each of these are given a cultivar name by the breeder or person who discovered that plant. Similarly with the hundreds of different hostas and dozens of different red maple trees, cultivars are all around us.

Cultivar names may reflect the person who found or bred the given plant, however, few people name plants after themselves. In the case of many of the stories told here, the names were provided by friends or nurseryman to whom the plant was given and by so doing, commemorated the individual or place where it was found.

Allan M. Armitage
October, 2001

ANNA, ILLINOIS

Anna, Illinois

Hydrangea arborescens 'Annabelle'

A nnabelle hydrangea is one of the most well known and beloved shrubs in American gardening. The name suggests there is an Anna in this plant's history, but she is a town instead of a person. The town is Anna, Illinois, and we have Joseph C. McDaniel to thank for the story of the discovery of *Hydrangea arborescens* 'Annabelle.'

According to Michael Dirr, who was a colleague of McDaniel's on the horticulture faculty of the University of Illinois, McDaniel portrayed the image of a dapper, if somewhat eccentric, English don, always wearing a fine coat and bow tie. Often this well-dressed figure could be seen driving down the streets of Urbana, Illinois, shovel and plants overhanging the rear of his ancient vehicle. He was a true gentleman and a plantsman of the highest order. Dirr credits him as being one of the finest American plant introducers of the twentieth century.

McDaniel described the history of his introduction of 'Annabelle' in a report to the International Plant Propagators' Society meeting in December 1962. When he first found the plant in Urbana, in 1960, he traced its origin back to Anna,

1

Illinois, where he spoke with a gentleman by the name of Hubbard Kirkpatrick. Kirkpatrick told McDaniel that his mother, Harriet, first saw the original plant in 1910. The spectacular flowers caught her attention while she was horseback riding on a wooded trail in the hills of Union County. When she returned to Anna she asked her sister, Amy, if she had ever seen a hydrangea with a "snowball" bloom. The two women realized the plant was special and collected it for their garden on Chestnut Street. Fifty years later, McDaniel reported he found clumps of the original plant still growing in the Chestnut Street garden.

During those 50 years the plant had been passed along by gardeners but had never been put into commercial production. The Kirkpatricks had talked about their plant with the Burpee Seed Company in Philadelphia, but found Burpee was more interested in a hydrangea called 'Snowhill.' McDaniel, however, thought the hydrangea from Anna had the largest and most symmetrical flower heads of all of the mutants from the wild, and he believed it should be made more widely available.

In 1960 he registered it as 'Annabelle' and convinced nurseries to grow and sell the plant. He stated it could be propagated as easily as any hydrangea, from dormant wood or greenwood leafy cuttings. 'Annabelle' first appeared in the catalogue of Albert B. Ferguson's Linn County Nurseries, Center Point, Iowa, in 1962.

The hydrangea's namesake town is located in southern Illinois. It was founded by Winsted Davie in 1850 and named for his wife, Anna. An agricultural community, Anna, Illinois, has a population of around 5,000. Before it became known for being the location of the original 'Annabelle,' its name was associated with a significant late-nineteenth-century stoneware pottery, the Anna Pottery, recognized for eccentric and humorous novelty wares. The owner of the pottery was Cornwall Kirkpatrick, the father of Harriet and Amy and grandfather of Hubbard, who shared the history of Annabelle with McDaniel.

H. arborescens is native to a large area of the United States, from New York south to Florida and Louisiana, and west to

Iowa, including southern Illinois. The woodlands that are now part of the Shawnee National Forest near Anna were probably the site of the original plant. The inflorescences of the species are mostly flattish and dull white, comprised of non-showy fertile flowers with a few sterile bracts. It is easy to see why 'Annabelle,' with its large round flower heads, caught the attention of the "Belles of Anna." Gardeners should not only thank the sisters for their discovery, but also sing the praises of the plantsman extraordinaire J. C. McDaniel for making this wonderful shrub available.

Reference

McDaniel, Joseph C. *International Plant Propagators' Society Proceedings*. 1962: 110-114.

Acknowledgments
Michael Dirr
Greg Mathis

Photograph courtesy of Leon O'Daniel—O'Daniel Designs (Kent, WA).

ARNOLD ARBORETUM

Logo of the Arnold Arboretum, Jamaica Plain, Massachusetts

Hamamelis x *intermedia* 'Arnold Promise'

The Arnold Arboretum is a hallowed name in United States horticulture, and, on the global list of arboreta and botanic gardens, remains one of the most highly regarded appellations. A plant bearing the mantle of this greatly respected institution must imply a highly desirable specimen. Indeed, *Hamamelis* 'Arnold Promise' has been recognized not only as an outstanding witch-hazel, but as "one of the finest shrubs ever to originate on its [the Arnold's] grounds."

This acclaimed witch-hazel is the result of a selection from seedlings collected in 1928 from the base of Chinese witch-hazel (*H. mollis*) by the Arnold's propagator William Judd. The Chinese witch-hazel was one grown from seeds collected in China in 1905 by the famous plant hunter E. H. Wilson. Judd observed the seedlings and, of the many sown, only seven reached maturity. The seven shrubs appeared to be hybrids of the Chinese witch-hazel and a nearby Japanese witch-hazel (*H. japonica*). In 1944, Alfred Rehder named the hybrid *Hamamelis* x *intermedia*.

A seedling from the Judd collection, the original 'Arnold Promise,' is planted on the southwest side of the Arboretum's administration building where, each year as winter fades, the profuse display of exceptionally large and fragrant flowers always attracts attention. Blessed with the fragrance and flowers of the Chinese combined with the cold hardiness of the Japanese, the plant inherited the best qualities of each parent. An especially well-formed vase-shaped shrub, ultimately 20' tall, the plant also attracts attention due to its outstanding yellow autumn foliage. This vigorous and spectacular witch-hazel chosen to bear the elite name of the Arnold Arboretum was registered on September 13, 1963.

To explain the Arnold Arboretum's legendary stature, it is necessary to refer to its remarkable history. Its origins are rooted in the fortunate bequest of a wealthy New Bedford, Massachusetts merchant, James Arnold. When he died in 1868, he left a portion of his estate in trust to three gentlemen, one being his nephew George Burrell Emerson, author of *Trees and Shrubs of Massachusetts* published in 1850. The trust stipulated that the money was to be used "for the promotion of Agricultural or Horticultural improvement," or, whatever philanthropic purpose the majority of the three men thought would represent the wishes of the deceased. Two of the men were interested in trees and decided to establish an institution for their study. To insure the permanence of this new place, the heirs turned to the Trustees and President and Fellows of Harvard College. In an agreement signed March 29, 1872, Harvard received the Arnold endowment and committed 125 acres of land, previously called the Bussey Farm, to become the Arnold Arboretum. In November 1873, Charles Sprague Sargent became its first director.

The dedication and leadership of Sargent molded the Arnold into the prestigious institution it was to become. Although there was little vision concerning the arboretum at the time, Sargent took on the assignment and, according to E. H. Wilson in his book *America's Greatest Garden, The Arnold Arboretum* (1925), Sargent's "hope and enthusiasm combined with untiring energy, unflinching resolve and doggedness of purpose" changed the Bussey Farm into today's arboretum. Stephen Spongberg, in his *Reunion of Trees* (1990), notes that Sargent "almost single-handedly established a living collection of American trees at the Arboretum."

Satisfied with his start on the collection of native American trees and shrubs, Sargent turned to investigating Asian flora and went to Japan to collect specimens and seeds for the Arnold. Subsequently, he arranged for plant collecting in China and convinced Wilson to take on the expeditions. During Sargent's 50 years at the Arnold, the arboretum explored almost every continent on earth and became the repository of numerous treasures.

The original 125-acre Bussey Farm, with its hills and valleys, fields and meadows, and steep cliffs, afforded interesting landscape backdrops for the cultivation of trees and shrubs. The arboretum today has grown to 265 acres and functions under the park system in the Jamaica Plain section of the city of Boston. The expanding arboretum is the result of a fortuitous linking of the visions of two men, Frederick Law Olmsted, a landscape architect working in 1873 on the Emerald Necklace park system for Boston, and Sargent, who was developing the Arboretum at the same time. Together they incorporated the Arnold into the network of parks, assuring it would have a system of walks and roads maintained by the city of Boston. In exchange, the university would assure the arboretum was open to the public. In conjunction with his work on the park system, Olmsted also suggested landscape designs for the new plant collections.

Sargent realized there was a need to inform those interested in learning of the Arnold's accomplishments. In 1888 he created a weekly newsletter from the arboretum called *Garden and Forest, A Journal for Horticulture Landscape Art and Forestry*, a publication he continued for 10 years. Today the Arnold publishes a quarterly magazine, *Arnoldia*, which chronicles the developments at the arboretum and contains articles about plant science, ecology, and related topics.

Arnoldia first reported the registration of *Hamamelis* x *intermedia* 'Arnold Promise' in Volume 28, Number 9, October 25, 1963, almost a century after Sargent began his program of plant collections, the work that eventually led to the discovery of this fine plant. Since the introduction of 'Arnold Promise' (often mislabeled as 'Arnold's Promise'), it has become one of the best known and most widely grown of all witch-hazels. Its pedigree and horticultural attributes make it an impressive plant for all seasons, and an outstanding tribute to its namesake.

References

Spongberg, Stephen A. *A Reunion of Trees.* Cambridge: Harvard University Press, 1990.

Weaver, Jr., Richard E. "Hamamelis 'Arnold Promise." *Arnoldia* 41 (1) 1981:30-31.

Wilson, Ernest H. *America's Greatest Garden, The Arnold Arboretum.* Boston: The Stratford Company, 1925.

Wyman, Donald. "New Plants Registered." *Arnoldia* 23 (9) October 25, 1963:111.

Acknowledgment

Carol David

Copy of the logo of the Arnold Arboretum courtesy of Joseph Melanson.

JANE BATH

Jane Bath

Dianthus gratianopolitanus 'Bath's Pink'

Jane Bath was surprised when she opened the 1983 catalogue from Goodness Grows Nursery in Crawford, Georgia, and found a listing for *Dianthus* 'Bath's Pink.' Several years before, she had discovered the plant and given it to her friends who owned the nursery, Rick Berry and Marc Richardson, for their evaluation. She was completely unaware however, they had named this special dianthus for her (Jane points out that Bath is her married name and muses about what might have been if her husband's name were other than an easy-to-remember four letter word!). A superior plant with a simple name, 'Bath's Pink' has become widely known and grown in the United States and Great Britain. Berry and Richardson thank Jane for bringing the plant to them, and credit her with the ability to recognize strong and durable plants.

Jane Bath grew up in Rehoboth, Georgia, a small town east of Atlanta. She loved flowers as a child and grew them in her own garden, coming to love the old-fashioned pinks most of all. When she discovered there were many varieties of pinks, she visited local garden centers and ordered by mail all that she could find. The young gardener developed her own trial garden and some of her pinks performed better than others, even in the same garden conditions. In what she refers to as her "trialing" period of life, she learned to recognize the value of selecting tough plants.

Jane received a degree in history from Emory University and married after college. The following 12 years, she and her husband lived in four cities outside the state of Georgia, and Jane made a garden at every home. When they returned to their home state, they moved to Stone Mountain, a suburb of Atlanta.

While creating her garden at her new home, Jane noticed a dianthus that just "wouldn't quit" growing at her neighbor's. Upon closer inspection, she found the compact, needlelike, gray-green foliage remained evergreen and discovered that the fragrance of its light pink flowers was the lovely scent of cloves. To Jane this plant seemed indestructible, even in rather brutal conditions. As a keen gardener with a broad knowledge of this genus, she realized it was a special plant, a plant that "worked" and quickly recognized its value By sharing it with Goodness Grows, Jane guaranteed its availability to all gardeners.

Like the plant that bears her name, Jane Bath possesses never-ending energy. After raising two daughters and a son, she returned to school and studied landscape design at South DeKalb College in Atlanta. She presently runs her own garden center, Land Arts, in Monroe, Georgia, where she focuses on lesser-known species. With great enthusiasm she often gives lectures about underused plants and writes about them in the newsletter she publishes for Land Arts. As an accomplished landscape designer in the southeast, she incorporates uncommon plants into her landscapes, and has no problem recommending 'Bath's Pink'. When she has a quiet moment, she works on her book of one-sentence theorems relating to the principles of design. This industrious woman also finds time to enjoy her family, especially her two young grandsons, Bailey and Brady.

Jane continues to look for vigorous plants and she has

passed along to Goodness Grows another discovery, a late-blooming fall aster. She hopes that, just as *Dianthus* 'Bath's Pink' did, this new plant will find its way into nursery catalogues and American gardens. Meanwhile, her namesake pink has been highlighted in several gardening magazines and continues to be celebrated for both its beauty and endurance.

Acknowledgments
Jane Bath
Rick Berry
Marc Richardson

Photograph courtesy of Jane Bath.

LOIE BENEDICT

Loie Benedict

Pulmonaria 'Benediction'

Visitors to Loie Benedict's garden quickly realized her almost sacred devotion to plants and experienced a beautiful haven that thrived under her tutelage. From her childhood on a farm near Arlington, Washington, to her present home in Auburn, Washington, her life spans most of the twentieth century. Her heartwarming philosophy and her gardening style have made her an inspiration to many.

The name of the *Pulmonaria* 'Benediction' honors Loie Benedict. Her friend Jerry Flintoff, a well-known gardener in the Pacific Northwest, discovered the lungwort in Loie's garden. He "noted it growing near a clump of the common form of *Pulmonaria angustifolia*...and it differed principally by the spotted leaves, otherwise being much like the putative seed parent." He doubted whether it is a cross with another Pulmonaria. But no matter its origin, it is an impressive lungwort. Its beauty is attributed mainly to its dark blue-green, lanceolate leaves marked with distinctive silver spots. Its flowers are dark blue and unfurl in the late spring. Flintoff named it *Pulmonaria* 'Benediction' and gave it to John Whittlesey at Canyon Creek Nursery in Oroville, California, to be propagated and marketed.

Loie Benedict was born on October 14,1907, one of four girls and eight boys. The family lived in rural Washington on a farm where they grew their food. Her father and brothers were loggers. Loie identified with her older brothers and participated with them in their more physically demanding tasks, occasionally even joining them on their logging trips. There were few social occasions in Loie's youth, but she fondly remembers parties after haying season, and still associates her family's Christmas celebrations with the smell of apples and oranges.

Her parents, who lacked formal education, nevertheless raised Loie to always respect nature and seek answers to her questions, guidance which led to her passionate love of books. Childhood trips to the woods with her mother taught her about wildflowers and instilled in Loie a keen interest in plants. She enrolled in the University of Washington to study botany, but fell victim to the burden of combining studying with working at the same time to pay for her education and left the university in her junior year.

During the following twenty years, Loie worked at many jobs with her husband Verne and moved to California. When the Depression subsided at the beginning of World War II, the Benedicts returned to Washington. In 1942, they purchased the home in Auburn where Loie still lives. Amazingly, it is located within a couple of miles of a logging site she visited as a child. When the Benedicts arrived in Auburn, the area was still undeveloped, and nothing resembling a garden was apparent at their new house. Loie began clearing the property of its rocks and blackberry vines. The strenuous physical labor, however, resulted in serious back problems and, ultimately, surgery. At the conclusion of a long and painful ordeal, she made a major decision.

Loie returned to school at the age of 48, and earned a degree as an occupational therapist. In so doing, she became the only one of the 12 children in her family to graduate from college. Her specialty became psychiatric occupational therapy, working with mentally ill patients. Describing Loie as a warm and caring person well-suited to this work, Jerry Flintoff has enjoyed boasting that she has been his own personal therapist for years.

Throughout her career as a therapist, Loie continued her enthusiasm for collecting and growing plants. Although Verne was not as passionate as she, Loie acknowledges her husband's support for her gardening efforts. Verne Benedict, according to Loie, was not a plant person, but "he even liked one or two of them." When he became ill in 1969, she retired from her professional work to care for him. After he died in 1975, she did not go back to her career, but began to complete the development of her garden. She worked in it full time for the next two decades, until she felt she could no longer keep up with its daily needs. Then Loie retired and returned her garden to Mother Nature.

Loie 's "full time" gardening consisted of six to ten hours per day, usually working alone and seldom stopping for lunch. Although constantly in pain from her back problems, she found that her best medicine was being surrounded by the plants she loved. With an emotional attachment to them and a bond of respect, she marveled at their endless variation. For her, each individual plant possesses its own personality and requirements. Meticulously she studied, examined, and noted her plants' idiosyncrasies. Watching a plant growing from seed to maturity has been one of her greatest joys. Loie's garden provided her enormous pleasure and was a reflection of her philosophy of life.

With her own hands Loie Benedict created a garden of unbridled beauty. She blended her collection of wonderful plants into a natural harmony, not a formal garden plan. Many plants in her garden are cherished gifts from friends and bring her delight as she is reminded by them of special relationships and associations. The importance Loie gives her friendships is revealed by her claim that she is "famous for her friends." But, this energetic, caring woman is also famous for the lovely garden she created and the handsome *Pulmonaria* that bears her name.

Reference
Olwell, Carol. *Gardening from the Heart.* Berkeley: Antelope
Island Press, 1990.

Acknowledgments
Loie Benedict
Jerry Flintoff
Dan Hinkley

Photograph courtesy of Carol Olwell.

RAY BRACKEN

Ray Bracken

Magnolia grandiflora 'Bracken's Brown Beauty'

Ray Bracken has a favorite quote, "If I do nothing else in my lifetime but leave the world a good tree, I've done something." And like a man possessed, he worked to make it come true. He fulfilled that quote when he introduced *Magnolia grandiflora* 'Bracken's Brown Beauty,' a tree that has established itself as one of the most widely recognized magnolias in the market.

Although distinctions between cultivars of southern magnolia are often subtle, 'Bracken's Brown Beauty' is acclaimed for several reasons. Bracken's selection dependably grows to a dense pyramidal tree with many forked lateral branches. From May until September, the tree is adorned with creamy white, fragrant flowers at the tips of the branches. The shiny, dark green leaves with curled-under edges also enhance its beauty, but it is the rusty brown, feltlike coating on the undersides of the leaves that gives the plant its name. Both the leaves and flowers are smaller than typical southern magnolias, making it a finer-textured and more uniform landscape plant than other magnolias. Its upright habit and excellent growth character have also allowed it to be successfully used as a street tree. Because of its hardiness to -22F, it is one of the few southern magnolias useful in colder climates. Ease of transplanting, fungal resistance, and shade tolerance are other qualities associated with this fine plant.

Bracken first noticed the tree growing in his nursery blocks in 1965. Although it was only 2 feet tall, this three-year-old seedling was the only one in bloom among thousands of others. He tagged the young plant and watched it develop. Convinced the tree was superior, Bracken wanted to ensure that its fine qualities were maintained. In 1982, Michael Dirr of the University of Georgia visited Bracken's nursery and was shown the magnolia. Bracken happily remembers the impressed Dirr exclaiming, "Bracken's Brown Beauty is the most beautiful southern magnolia I have ever observed." Dirr suggested Bracken patent the plant and helped him supply the documentation necessary to prove the plant was distinctive. 'Bracken's Brown Beauty', was awarded plant patent No. 5520 in 1984, to last for twenty years.

The popularity of this outstanding tree has brought fame to the Ray Bracken Nursery. Located in Piedmont, South Carolina, the business dates to the years of the Great Depression. Hard times caused Ray's dad, Albert, to lose his South Carolina farm and search for another means of income. He left his family in Liberty, South Carolina and joined his brother-in-law in the business of buying and selling large trees that were being dug from old plantation properties in North Carolina. With a fleet of four pickup trucks and the help of able-bodied men who worked for food, the brothers loaded one tree onto each truck and headed for Washington, D.C. If they did not sell the trees there, they went on to Baltimore, then as far north as Philadelphia if necessary. However, Mr. Bracken soon missed his wife and ten children and returned home to South Carolina and became a sharecropper. The tree business however, remained in his blood.

While working as a gardener on weekends he once again found a way grow and sell trees. He dug a large earthen pit, and rooted the pruned cuttings from his gardening jobs. Those cuttings became the first trees of the nursery Mr. Bracken opened in 1936. In 1958, Ray Bracken followed his father's lead and opened Ray Bracken Nursery, Inc. which now includes a division in Georgia.

Ray Bracken has retired, but he has two great horticultural accomplishments to his credit. He has given the world a good tree and developed a fine nursery. The business, now being run by three of Bracken's four children, is a far cry from his father's tree-selling operation during the Great Depression. Large digging equipment and enormous wire baskets were not even imagined in the days of the four pick-up trucks. And, neither was a tree so fine as the uniquely beautiful and adaptable southern magnolia Ray Bracken has given the world.

References

Davis, Todd. "Protecting New Varieties." *NMPro* September 1998: 29-31.

Dirr, Michael A. "Southern Magnolia Introduces Beauty, Hardiness to the Landscape." *Nursery Manager* July 1991: 34-35.

Kellum, Jo. "The Magnolia." *Southern Living* May, 1996: 116-117.

Acknowledgments

Ray Bracken
Teresa Bracken

Photograph courtesy of Teresa Bracken.

LUTHER BURBANK

Luther Burbank

Rosa 'Burbank'

Luther Burbank was known as the "Plant Wizard" of Santa Rosa. He focused his life on improving plants and made several hundred introductions to horticulture. Although he is associated with many new plants, only one ornamental was given the Burbank name. This special honor went to his favorite flower, a rose, which was appropriately named *Rosa* 'Burbank.'

Burbank describes the origin of his rose in *Luther Burbank; His Methods and Discoveries and Their Practical Applications*, his 12-volume treatise about his work. The 'Burbank' rose started from rarely produced seeds of a Bourbon rose (Hermosa species) which Burbank then crossed with other parents to introduce "new blood" into his hybrids. Because the records of Burbank's work are notoriously lacking, the identities of the many parents are unknown, but in his hybridizing process, Burbank developed a rose with improved qualities in hardiness and productivity. His resulting Burbank rose was also fragrant, a perpetual bloomer, and a vigorous grower, as well as being highly resistant to mildew and rust. In addition to those qualities, the natural beauty of the flowers was enhanced by petals with rolled-back edges. Burbank considered his rose significantly better than any other and used it to exemplify how increased vigor and variation result from cross-fertilization.

The rose was introduced in 1900. It became extremely popular and won a Gold Medal as the best bedding rose at the St. Louis Exposition in 1904. Burbank noted with great pride that "competent judges everywhere have admitted that it deserved the recognition." In the United States, *Rosa* 'Burbank' is still available in several specialty rose nurseries, all of which report Burbank's claims are indeed true.

Luther Burbank's accomplishments in horticulture may be traced to his early life. He was born in Lancaster, Massachusetts, on March 7, 1849. His English-born father gave him an appreciation for books and learning, and his Scottish-born mother gave him an appreciation for beauty. Luther attended school in Lancaster but gained much of his education from reading books on science and nature. Two contemporary authors had a profound influence on his thinking: Ralph Waldo Emerson, a family friend, inspired the young Burbank with his philosophy of self-reliance, and Charles Darwin, through his book *On the Variation of Animals and Plants under Domestication* (1868), led Burbank to explore methods of artificial selection in plant breeding.

While Burbank was still in school he worked for the Ames Plow Company in Worcester and demonstrated exceptional engineering abilities. But engineering of another kind came to light as his true calling in 1870, after he purchased his own farm in Lunenburg, Massachusetts. While observing a crop of potatoes, Burbank noticed a great deal of variation in the tops of the plants, and on one plant he even found viable seeds, rarely produced by field grown potatoes. From his observation and discovery, he developed the famous Burbank potato. This large, hardy variety—a great improvement over the small, easily spoiled ones grown at that time—became the building block of today's well-known baker, the "Idaho."

After suffering heat stroke on the farm in Massachusetts,

Burbank decided to find his future in the more temperate climate of California. In 1875, at age 25, he moved to a rural area 50 miles north of San Francisco, now known as Santa Rosa. Following a period of hard times and hard work, he finally saved enough money to purchase land and establish a nursery business, which he ran for seven years. However, he was not able to spend enough time on developing new plants, so in 1893, he closed his successful nursery to focus on breeding.

Burbank's reputation grew as he improved fruits, vegetables, nuts, and grains, among them the Santa Rosa plum and Santa Rosa artichoke. Of the many ornamentals he produced he is best known for the popular shasta daisy, a plant that helped the ornamental industry expand and succeed. Many nurseries still refer to the shasta as the Burbank daisy. One of Burbank's highly publicized introductions was the spineless cactus. He intended it to be used as cattle fodder; however, because of its low nutritional value it was never accepted.

Burbank's many creations were brought to public attention by his plant introduction catalogue, *New Creations in Fruits and Flowers*, published annually between 1893 and 1901. His catalogue became widely acclaimed, and plant orders from around the globe arrived at Burbank's Experiment Farms in Santa Rosa.

In 1905, as Burbank's fame increased and the results of his experiments were celebrated, he was recognized by Tufts College with an honorary Doctor of Science degree. The same year he received an annual grant of $5,000 from the Carnegie Institution. However, because Burbank was never particularly interested in finances and resisted paying attention to the rigors of keeping scientific data, he and the Carnegie Institution parted ways in 1910.

In spite of deficiencies in formal education and record keeping, he was a complete master at what he did. Burbank crossed and recrossed plants to produce untold variations from which he could select those with the greatest vigor and yield. According to Hugo de Vries's 1907 monograph, *Plant Breeding*, Burbank, through his empirical methods and keen observations of plant attributes, laid the foundation for applied botanical genetics.

While Burbank's honorary degree may have appropriately recognized his contribution to the science of plant breeding, no laws existed at the time to protect his introductions. Consequently, Luther Burbank received no personal wealth for his achievements and many of his creations were stolen by others. Federal legislation protecting plant breeders with patents similar to those for other types of inventions finally passed after Burbank's death.

Through the Luther Burbank Press, established in 1912 in conjunction with the Luther Burbank Society, Burbank directed the writing of the 12 volumes of *Methods and Discoveries* and wrote the 8-volume *How Plants are Trained to Work for Man*. Burbank's work became so well known that the verb "burbank," meaning "to modify and improve by selective breeding," or, simply, "to make something better," was included in standard American dictionaries in the 1940s.

Luther Burbank waited until he was 67 years old to marry. Elizabeth Waters, his former secretary, who was not quite 30 at the time, became his wife. They were happily married for the last 10 years of Burbank's life and she never remarried, always claiming Luther Burbank was the only man who made her "feel like a million dollars."

Luther and Elizabeth lived on four acres of property in Santa Rosa, which she inherited at the time of his death. In 1960, Elizabeth gave half of their property to the city, and at her death in 1977, the remaining property and buildings were also bequeathed to the city to become a living museum, the Luther Burbank Home and Gardens. Santa Rosa has always been proud of Luther Burbank and, continuing a tradition begun during his lifetime, the city celebrates the third weekend in May every year by producing the Luther Burbank Rose Parade.

Burbank's life was never dull, and he did not shun controversy. In 1926, during the decade of the Scopes trial as well as Henry Ford's declaration supporting reincarnation, Burbank was interviewed about his position on religion. The interview resulted in the appearance of a front-page story in the *San Francisco Bulletin* with the headline, "'I'm an Infidel' Declares Burbank, Casting Doubt on Soul Immortality Theory." The story caused shockwaves around the globe, and Burbank was inundated with calls and mail from supporters and critics alike and spent grueling hours responding to these messages. Perhaps because of the long hours he spent defending himself, his health deteriorated. On March 26, 1926, he suffered a heart attack and died on April 11th.

In spite of the controversy at the end of his life, an estimated 10,000 people attended Burbank's memorial service where Judge Ben Lindsey, a friend from Denver, Colorado, paid him tribute, saying that Burbank "would be forever known as one of the world's greatest benefactors. In the creative improvement of plant life, he is our greatest genius."

Burbank requested he be buried in an unmarked grave beneath a cedar of Lebanon beside the door to his cottage. The tree has since died, but all around the house and gardens are many reminders of the life work of one of America's most extraordinary plantsmen. Luther Burbank's introductions, including his wonderful Burbank rose, forever enriched the world's cornucopia of plants.

References

Barker, Dan. "The Forgotten Story of Luther Burbank." *Freethought Today* August, 1993: 2-7 .

Burbank, Luther. *Luther Burbank: His Methods and Discoveries, Their Practical Application*, Vol. IX. New York: Luther Burbank Press, 1914.

Encyclopedia of World Biography, 2nd ed. 17 vols. Gale Research. 1998.

Harwood, W. S. *New Creations in Plant Life: An Authoritative Account of the Life and Work of Luther Burbank*. New York: Grosset & Dunlap, 1907.

Toth, Susan Allen. "The Father of Invention, Luther Burbank, Plant Wizard." *Garden Design* October, 1998: 59-61+.

Acknowledgments
Pierre Bennerup
Blanche Farley
Bill Patterson

Photograph courtesy of Cathy Stevenson, Luther Burbank Home & Gardens, Santa Rosa, California.

MOLLY BUSH

Molly Bush

Heuchera 'Molly Bush'

It is a well-known fact that fathers have a special place in their hearts for their daughters. When Allen Bush was asked by a Dutch nurseryman to provide a name for the distinctive *Heuchera*, commonly called coral bells, from his North Carolina nursery, he immediately thought of his 11-year-old little girl, Molly, the apple of his eye.

Allen Bush, a Kentuckian by birth, graduated from the University of Kentucky in 1973. His degree was in sociology, but he found his calling in the world of plants. Five years after college he went to the Royal Botanic Gardens, Kew, England, as an international trainee, an experience that sealed his future in horticulture. Upon his return to the United States, he purchased a farm in Fletcher, North Carolina and in 1980 opened Holbrook Farm Nursery, named for his mother's family.

Bush remained in touch with his colleagues at Kew and stayed abreast of the new plants in their collection. Tony Hall, supervisor of the Alpine House and Woodland Garden at Kew, sent him some seeds from a new purple-leaved coral bell called 'Palace Purple,' discovered at Kew on the grounds of the royal palace. From those seeds, Bush introduced the plant to U.S.

gardeners in 1986. 'Palace Purple' was such a hit in the United States that it was named Perennial Plant of the Year in 1991.

Over the years, Bush consistently reselected plants with even darker purple leaves from the original 'Palace Purple' plants. One of his selections with particularly dark, reddish bronze foliage caught the attention of some visiting European nurserymen, including Luk Klinkhamer from Holland and Klaus Jelitto from Germany, who requested some pieces of the new plant. Not long after, in a call from Holland Bush was told his discovery was being put into tissue culture propagation and needed a name for distribution. Without losing a beat, the proud nurseryman became the proud father and *Heuchera* 'Molly Bush' was born.

The parentage of 'Molly Bush' is undetermined and may be listed sometimes under *H. micrantha* or *H. americana*. Regardless of its taxonomic origin, its most distinguishing characteristic is the consistent dark purple color of its ivy-shaped leaves. Its small flowers are of little consequence but add contrast to the striking foliage.

Molly Bush was born in Fletcher, North Carolina, in 1981. When Allen Bush closed Holbrook Farm in 1995, he moved to Louisville, Kentucky. Molly joined him there in 1996. After she graduated from Louisville's Saint Francis High School in 2000, she enrolled in Eugene Lang, the liberal arts college of the New School, in New York City. During high school she participated in productions at Louisville's Walden Theater, a training program for serious young actors. Living in New York, this lovely young woman with light brown hair and green eyes may be headed for theatrical production rather than the plant production, but 'Molly Bush' is a center-stage plant that commemorates Molly and her father's contributions to horticulture.

Acknowledgment
Allen Bush

Photograph courtesy of Allen Bush.

CEDAR LANE FARM

Jane Symmes

Lonicera sempervirens 'Cedar Lane'

Cedar Lane Farm is located near Madison, Georgia, the lovely southern town that, according to legend, General Sherman found "too beautiful to burn" on his March to the Sea during the Civil War. John and Jane Symmes bought the property in 1966, and built a nursery worthy of its historical setting.

Both John and Jane grew up in Atlanta. John studied business at the University of Georgia, but after serving in the second World War attended the University of Florida to study horticulture. After he received his degree in 1947, he returned to Atlanta and began Symmes Nursery, a commercial landscape company.

Jane Campbell was also from Atlanta and graduated from Agnes Scott College where she majored in art history. Gardening, however had been an important part of her life and she fondly recalls visiting nurseries with her mother and meeting wonderful nursery people. After Jane graduated from college, she and her mother still visited nurseries together and on one occasion her mother asked Jane to accompany her to purchase a magnolia. As fate would have it, they visited Symmes

26

Nursery, and John helped make their selection. Mutual interests led to many more enjoyable meetings for Jane and John, and the encounter at the magnolia led to their marriage in 1956.

Not long after they were married, Jane filled in at the nursery for an absent secretary and from that time on worked closely with John. As the business prospered, John found himself more and more confined to the office and less free to be outside in the nursery. At the same time, he and Jane were finding that because of the limited selection of landscape plants, a large part of their work was searching for new and better plants for the nursery. In order to begin a nursery outside of the city and work outdoors with the plants, they hired someone to help run the landscape business in Atlanta. Thus, the search for land commenced.

With their new plan fresh in her mind, Jane happened to go on a garden tour to Madison which is 60 miles east of Atlanta. She admired the beautiful countryside and began to look for an available farm. A suitable one was found, but John decided time was too precious to be consumed by travel between Atlanta and Madison. However, two years later, when travel time was considerably shortened with the building of an interstate highway, they decided to reconsider purchasing the Madison farm. Not only was the land beautiful but was blessed with a natural spring, and included an 1830s "plantation plain" style house that could be restored. Without another thought, they purchased Cedar Lane Farm in 1966.

While making plans for the restoration of the house and its garden, John and Jane planted the first tree crops for the nursery, including cryptomerias and Norway spruces, plants little known in the South at that time. During those early years, they continued to live in Atlanta, but by1972, the nursery business had grown and they were about to move to the farm. Then, without warning, John was diagnosed with cancer. Eleven months later, at age 50, he died.

Jane was committed to the project she and John had begun,

27

but with two young daughters to support and educate, a nursery in Madison, and the landscape business in Atlanta, she faced enormous challenges. The economy was experiencing rapid inflation and rising interest rates, and there was financial uncertainty in the business community. Her challenges became even greater when the man she and John had hired to help in Atlanta quit because he would not work for a woman. Weighing her options, Jane sold the Atlanta operation and concentrated on the nursery. With dedicated hard work, she made Cedar Lane Farm one of the finest nurseries in the country. Other growers recognized her as a trendsetter in the industry and often called upon her for advice.

Historical plants became one focus for Cedar Lane Farm. When Jane became interested in restoring the garden around her house, she could not find any nurseries providing appropriate plants. She decided her nursery would be that source. From old seed catalogues and early garden literature, she gathered information, and in 1976, to mark the bicentennial of the United States, she distributed a Cedar Lane list called "Plant Material for Historic Gardens." The list became a valuable tool for garden restoration work, and Cedar Lane became nationally known as a source for native and historical plants. She counted among her customers many prominent historical gardens, including the one at Thomas Jefferson's Monticello.

As years went by, Cedar Lane became known for growing many kinds of plants and for introducing a number of them to the nursery trade. *Magnolia grandiflora* 'Symmes Select' resulted from a project started by John when the business was still only a dream. He had collected magnolia seeds from Westview Cemetery, an old cemetery in Atlanta, and planted them in a field at the Madison farm. A large crop of seedlings resulted, from which he selected the best looking and strongest one, and made cuttings. Della Mae Johnson, Cedar Lane's propagator grew the rooted cuttings until they were introduced in the 1987 catalogue. The magnolia was named to honor John.

Jane's leadership of the nursery led to several other introductions. She believed that native honeysuckles, *Lonicera sempervirens*, were underused as garden plants, and began to grow them at Cedar Lane. She discovered one of her best specimens while walking the woods on her farm, a lovely plant with crimson-red trumpet flowers and clear blue-green foliage. Plants were propagated and 'Cedar Lane' honeysuckle was introduced in 1980. It has proven to be a particularly strong performer in the Southeast and a good selection for most American gardens. Many nurseries and public gardens, including Winterthur Gardens in Delaware, have promoted it.

Another honeysuckle offered by Cedar Lane was given to Jane by her friend Fred Thode, an outstanding plantsman and professor of landscape architecture at Clemson University. The beautiful clear yellow–flowered native honeysuckle came to Thode from a lady who discovered it in Oconee County, South Carolina. Jane was thrilled when Thode passed the plant on to her. She introduced it as *Lonicera sempervirens* 'Sulphurea' in 1979.

Long-time Madison resident Fannin Stokes was responsible for the Confederate jasmine that John and Jane later named for their new hometown. Not long after they bought their farm they were invited for dinner by Stokes. When they commented on the lovely, old jasmine vine growing on her raised cottage home, their hostess exclaimed that it had not frozen for one hundred years. Jane planted an offspring on her own chimney in 1970, and *Trachelospermum jasminoides* 'Madison' was born. Her chimney still supports this fragrant white-flowered vine that continues to flaunt its cold hardiness.

Not far from Madison is Athens, Georgia, a community where the Ladies' Garden Club, the first garden club in the United States, was founded in 1895, and a town where interest in gardening has long been a tradition. Two well-known names in the Athens garden community were Mrs. Wymberly DeRenne, a talented garden designer, and Mrs. Sewell Brumby,

29

an outstanding gardener. For many years, they had watched a remarkable yellow-flowered sweet shrub bloom beside an old home in the Five Points area of town. In 1964, when DeRenne and Brumby heard the house was to be torn down, they made plans to rescue the plant. Under the cover of darkness, these two upstanding ladies saved the sweetshrub from destruction and later shared it with their nursery friend, Jane Symmes. The origin of the plant is not known, but there is speculation that it came to the Athens garden from the former Fruitlands Nursery, the present location of the Augusta (Georgia) National Golf Club. Appearing in the nursery's 1859 catalogue is a listing for a light-colored sweet shrub. Jane named the rescued shrub *Calycanthus floridus* 'Athens' for the wonderful town where it was saved. Its consistently fragrant yellow flowers, and exceptional dark green foliage have made it a popular garden plant.

In 1987, daughter Jeanne, who had studied at the New York Botanic Garden after college, joined her mother in running the nursery. Jane and Jeanne enjoyed working together and made many friends in the industry, but in 1995 they decided to close the business and point their lives in a new direction. For 29 years, under the guidance of a fine plantswoman, Cedar Lane Farm made significant contributions to American gardens.

Jane Symmes continues to live at Cedar Lane Farm where she maintains several gardens surrounding her beautifully restored home, including an enclosed boxwood parterre, a perennial border, and a kitchen garden. On a hillside beside the house, she is developing an extensive woodland garden adjacent to spring-fed ponds. In the gardens and along the walks Jane has carefully placed many of the fine plants she introduced from Cedar Lane Farm, her much-missed nursery.

References

Samuels, Ellen, and Rosemary Verey. *The American Woman's Garden*. Boston: Little Brown & Company, 1984.

Symmes, Mrs. John C. *Plant Material for Historic Gardens*. Madison: Cedar Lane Farms, 1975.

Acknowledgments
Rick Crown
Jane Symmes
Jeanne Symmes

Photograph courtesy of Jane Symmes.

JOHN CHAMPNEYS, PHILLIPPE NOISETTE

Noisette Rose Garden, Charleston, South Carolina

Rosa 'Champneys' Pink Cluster'
Rosa 'Blush Noisette'

Throughout history, the rose has been a beloved garden flower. In the early 1800s, roses enjoyed enormous popularity in French gardens, and came to be fashionably and horticulturally associated with that country. One of the most famous gardens of the time was the rose garden of Empress Josephine at Chateau de la Malmaison. Indulging her passion for roses, she collected more than two hundred varieties. When the botanical painter, Pierre Joseph Redouté published *Les Roses* in 1824, he included many engravings of flowers from Malmaison and forever connected the rose with the French state.

Acknowledging France as the early epicenter for rose cultivation, it may come as a surprise to learn that the well-known class of roses which bears the French name "Noisette" was developed in a garden near Charleston, South Carolina. 'Champneys' Pink Cluster', the first Noisette rose, was hybridized by John Champneys in his plantation garden southwest of Charleston shortly after 1800. Because the plantation's book of records for that time is lost, the exact date cannot be determined, but the parents of Champneys' rose are known, and it is possible to piece together the story of the rose's discovery.

Born in South Carolina, December 28, 1743, the son of a British official, John Champneys remained a Loyalist and was a successful wharfinger at the time of the American Revolution. As a result of his refusal to take the oath of allegiance as requested by the 1776 South Carolina Provincial Congress, he experienced a brief imprisonment, loss of family, and generally an unsettled life of travel between the colonies and England until 1790, when, according to notes in his gardening diary, he returned to Charleston in the newly established United States of America.

In 1796, Champneys purchased a 26-acre estate on the Wallace River south of Charleston formerly owned by William Williamson. It was described in David Ramsay's *History of South Carolina* (1809) as "...one of the most elaborate early gardens... in St. Paul's district..." This description indicates Champneys enjoyed gardening and was likely involved with the plants growing there, including the roses. It is well documented that Champneys hybridized the pink flowering one later given his name.

The parents of Champneys' hybrid, *Rosa moschata* (the Musk rose) and *Rosa chinensis* (Old Blush rose)are known, but there are several theories about how Champneys acquired them. The musk rose, with clusters of highly fragrant double or single white flowers, had long been grown in English gardens and most probably was already growing in the Williamson garden when Champneys purchased the plantation. However, the musk rose does not perform well when planted in the hot climate of the American Southeast. The other parent, the China rose 'Old Blush', or 'Parson's Pink China', performs quite well in the southern climate and is noteworthy for its long blooming season. It is likely that Champneys ordered 'Old Blush' directly from the William Prince Nursery in Flushing Landing, New York

(Prince's catalogue made the first U.S. reference to 'Old Blush' in 1799). By crossing the two roses, Champneys produced a rose hybrid that combines the desirable traits of both species. With its large clusters of fragrant light pink semi-double flowers that appear from June until November, his new rose was the first truly reblooming rose of the Western world. However, Champneys' contribution to the world of roses went mostly uncelebrated by his contemporaries even though it came to be called by his name.

The story continues with a Frenchman, Phillippe Noisette, who moved to Charleston at the beginning of the nineteenth century. The son of a gardener to French royalty, Noisette fled the French Revolution and, being a horticulturist, was lured through botanical interests to Charleston. He became the director of the Botanical Society of Charleston, the first botanical society and garden founded in the United States. However, the society fell on hard times and within a few years was out of existence. Having previously begun a nursery, Noisette became its full time proprietor.

By 1817, the Champneys rose journeyed to France. According to William Prince's son, Robert, in *Manual of Roses* (1846), "The old Blush Noisette Rose was raised...by Phillippe Noisette, of Charleston, from seed of the Champneys' rose, and this he sent to his brother Louis Noisette of Paris, under the name of the Noisette Rose." When the two flowers are compared, 'Blush Noisette' is blush pink, fully double, with larger and more refined petals than Champneys' rose. Louis Noisette realized the importance of the Noisette rose and suggested Redouté draw the flower. Thus, the newest rose sensation was immortalized, as was the Noisette name, which ultimately designated an entire class of roses.

'Champneys' Pink Cluster' was popular in American gardens throughout the nineteenth century. According to Robert Buist's *The American Flower Garden Directory* (1832), "This celebrated rose has a situation in almost every garden in our city [Philadelphia], and forms a great ornament, flowering very profusely in immense clusters from May to November...one of the most abundant in flower, the easiest of culture, (growing in any exposure) and in every respect is highly deserving of attention." All of the Noisette roses (the descendents of the Champneys' rose developed in France by Louis Noisette, particularly Phillippe's 'Blush Noisette') received considerable attention at the time. However, by the mid twentieth-century, tea roses had become the fashion and the Noisettes could be found only in old gardens and cemeteries.

A resurgence of interest in old roses in the late twentieth century brought attention once again to the Noisette roses. Their graceful nature makes them worthy garden additions, well suited for training on pergolas, pillars, walls, and arbors. Generally fragrant, their handsome pastel flowers bloom in profusion in the late spring and magically reappear in the fall. To verify their newfound popularity and showcase their beauty, many varieties of Noisette roses have recently been planted in display gardens, such as the Léonie Bell Noisette Rose Garden at the Center for Historic Plants adjacent to Monticello in Charlottesville, Virginia.

Another Noisette rose garden was planted near Charleston, the site of the 2001 International Heritage Rose Conference. It is an excellent display garden dedicated to the study of this class of roses. The city of Charleston, acknowledging its place in horticultural history, designated 'Champneys' Pink Cluster' as its official rose and volunteers have planted the Noisette Rose Trail that features the roses at 18 public sites around the city.

John Champneys died in 1820 and, with his rose planted beside his grave, rests in peace in the churchyard of St. Phillips in Charleston. His heirs moved from South Carolina and unfortunately, nothing remains of his garden, nor is any painting of his likeness known to exist. Phillippe Noisette's heirs, however, continued the family's long and celebrated existence even after he died in 1835. Until the middle of the twentieth century, Charlestonians depended on "The Rose Garden" at Charleston Neck to supply their special-occasion roses. Noisette's unmarked grave is thought to rest in the churchyard of St. Mary's Catholic Church in Charleston.

John Champneys and Phillippe Noisette participated in some of the most significant events in the development of the rose. The roses that bear their names pay tribute to them and commemorate an important chapter in American horticulture.

References

Austin, Glenn. "The Noisettes: Roses With Southern Heritage." *Perennial Notes* Summer 1997:11-12.

Cornett, Peggy. "'Champneys Pink Cluster' Comes to Monticello." *Twin Leaf* 1999: 9-13.

Cornett, Peggy. "The Léonie Bell Noisette Rose Garden at Monticello." *Magnolia, Bulletin of the Southern Garden History Society* Winter/Spring 1990: 8.

Fitzpatrick, John T. "Study Gardens of Noisette Roses to be Planted in Fall 1998 for the 9th International Heritage Rose Conference." *Magnolia, Bulletin of the Southern Garden History Society* Summer 1998: 8.

Hash, C. Patton. "Champneys' Triumph: South Carolina's Forgotten Rose." *Carologue, A publication of the South Carolina Historical Society* Spring 2000: 8-16.

Seidel, Rev. Douglas. "Progress Report on the Bell Garden and Documentation of an Ancient Musk Rose." *Magnolia, Bulletin of the Southern Garden History Society* Winter/Spring 1990: 8.

Acknowledgments

Patty Alexander
Pat Hash
Alice Levkoff
Rita Donato

Photograph by Bill Murton.

CORBETT, MARYLAND

Andrew and Larry Clemens

Aquilegia canadensis 'Corbett'

Corbett, Maryland, is a small and closely knit community north of metropolitan Baltimore that was formerly a crossroads on the North Central Railroad line connecting Baltimore and Harrisburg, Pennsylvania. Originally a farm village with a post office, general store, and a saw mill, Corbett depended on the local "milk trains" to provide passenger service and supplies, and to transport the finished lumber.

Eventually the post office, the store, and the sawmill were closed and the trains no longer ran. The tracks were removed after the flood of Hurricane Flora in 1972. However, Corbett remains a quiet and peaceful place to live and raise a family. The wide flat railroad right of way has become a popular hiking and biking trail; the name "Corbett" marks the gate at Corbett Road.

The homes of Corbett portray their connection to the charm of the last century, and with the exception of two houses, all were built prior to 1900. Shirley Clemens still resides in the 1890 clapboard home at the top of Corbett Village Lane where she

37

and her husband raised their four sons. Just down the hill were the railroad tracks, the path to adventure for the boys. Along those tracks they explored and discovered nature, learned the native plants, and found their way to nearby Monkton for candy and soda.

Venturing down the railway path one day in the late 1960s, the two youngest Clemens boys, Andrew and Larry, discovered a hauntingly beautiful yellow-flowered columbine. They were young teenagers at the time, but familiar enough with the native columbine to know the light yellow flowers were quite different from the normal color of the species. They transplanted a sample to their mother's garden and enjoyed it for a couple of years, until it simply did not reappear one spring. Several years later, Andrew once again found the plant growing on the hillside along the tracks. This time he collected seeds and gave them to neighbors so that it would not be lost again.

One of the neighbors was Richard Simon, owner of Bluemount Nurseries in Monkton, Maryland. Simon was thrilled to receive the new columbine and wanted to propagate it for distribution. Through Richard Lighty at Mount Cuba Center, Simon verified the plant was "a chance seedling collected from the wild." He grew and studied the plants for several years, noting that the yellow columbines came true from seed. Simon asked the brothers to select a name for it. They insisted it not be their own, but chose 'Corbett,' forever immortalizing their hometown. In 1992, when Simon finally had sufficient numbers, he introduced Aquilegia canadensis 'Corbett' in the Bluemount Nurseries catalogue, approximately 25 years after it was originally found by the Clemens brothers. In 1993 Wayside Gardens included it in their catalogue, and since that time the plant has been widely available.

The beautiful nodding flowers of the native columbine of eastern North America are universal springtime favorites whether in the wild or in cultivated gardens. 'Corbett' is similar to the species in form, but is shorter and more compact and makes a dense mound covered in sulphur yellow flowers. The original plants seem to lose vigor and even disappear in a garden after three or four years, but they may reseed, and, thanks to Andrew, can now be replaced.

Andrew became a school teacher in Baltimore and Larry is a librarian at the Naval Academy, not surprising professions for these two men who displayed such a keen sense of observation in their youth. Their discovery of 'Corbett' has provided gardeners another handsome native plant to include among springtime treasures.

And perhaps along the hiking-biking path through Corbett in the springtime, there may still be a lovely pale yellow columbine on the hillside nodding proudly and awaiting recognition by other passersby.

References

Perry, L. P. "'Corbett' Columbine." HortScience 1995: 165.
Stiehm, Jamie. "Flower Find is Getting Popular." The Sun
September 12, 1997: 3B

Acknowledgments

Andrew Clemens
Shirley Clemens
Martha Simon Pindale
Richard Simon

Photograph courtesy of Shirley Clemens.

BETTY CORNING

Betty Corning

Clematis viticella 'Betty Corning'

Betty Corning simply enjoyed gardening. She enjoyed growing plants and sharing her hobby with others. Married to Erastus Corning II, the longest serving mayor of Albany, New York (from 1941 until he died in office in 1983), Betty was also well-known, and her position may have provided the entrée needed to acquire the plant that now bears her name. And for gardeners, 'Betty Corning' does not conjure up political plots and ambitions, but rather the name of a beautiful clematis vine.

Erastus and Elizabeth met in Northeast Harbor, Maine, where their families had neighboring summer homes. Betty's family, the Platts, was from Philadelphia, and the Cornings were an established political family in Albany. In 1932, when Betty was 20 years old, the couple married and moved into the house that one time was the gardener's cottage on the Corning estate called Corning Hill, in Albany.

The land surrounding their home was vacant and offered Betty the perfect opportunity to pursue her gardening passion. While her husband was busy being mayor, Betty spent her time developing the landscape into a beautiful garden. Her zeal was

40

not surprising; after all, she was the daughter of Mrs. Charles Platt, a passionate gardener in her own right and a founding member of The Garden Club of America.

On a summer day in 1933, Betty took her mother to see a remarkable clematis she had noticed growing across the porch of a house in the downtown area. Mrs. Platt, who was particularly knowledgeable about clematis, told her daughter that she had never seen such silvery lavender flowers on a clematis vine before. At her mother's insistence, but with a great deal of trepidation, Betty rang the doorbell to ask about the plant. The homeowner recognized her visitor instantly and was pleased, and perhaps honored, to share her plant. Betty dug a piece and when she asked about its history, Betty learned the woman had received it from a friend who had rooted it in a potato! Even though most people looked at her in disbelief, Betty always mentioned this fact when she was asked about the plant.

As it turned out, Corning had arrived at the downtown house just in time. Soon after she dug the plant, the house and its vine-covered porch succumbed to the bulldozer. Shortly thereafter, the property on Albany's Bertha Street became part of the Nelson A. Rockefeller Empire State Plaza, a government complex in Albany that, coincidentally, includes the Erastus Corning Tower.

Unaware she had saved a unique clematis from extinction, Betty took the rescued plant home to her garden. Over the years all who saw the vine were struck by the delicate beauty of its flowers and further impressed when told about its long blooming season. Betty finally agreed that it should be propagated and introduced. She sent samples to the Arnold Arboretum for study and found her mother had been right. In 1970, Theodore Dudley confirmed it was a new clematis hybrid and described and introduced *Clematis viticella* 'Betty Corning' in *The American Horticultural Magazine*, the publication of the American Horticultural Society. Its special qualities were further recognized when it received the Pennsylvania Horticultural Society's Gold Medal in 1992. Betty Corning was proud of her namesake and shared it with many botanical gardens and arboretums with the hope it would become more available to gardeners.

Elizabeth Platt Corning was from a refined Philadelphia background and was well prepared to become the first lady of Albany. Although she was disinterested in politics, she was involved in community service through a variety of organizations centering especially on her gardening passion, "Gardening is a way of life for me," she once said. "I can't imagine life without it." She was an ardent spokeswoman for community gardening and developed a successful beautification program for downtown neighborhoods called "Window Boxes for Better Blocks." She and other garden club members provided the window boxes and plants and helped inner city residents enjoy the beauty of flowers. Because of Betty's expertise and knowledge, she was often consulted on behalf of city projects concerning greenspace, plants, and conservation.

A tireless leader, Corning was also committed to numerous conservation and horticulture organizations that took her beyond the Albany community. She was president of the boards of the George Landis Arboretum in Esperance, New York, and the Berkshire Botanical Garden in Stockbridge, Massachusetts. She served on the boards of the American Horticultural Society, the Garden Conservancy, and the New York Botanical Garden. But Corning's greatest commitment was to The Garden Club of America, as a member of the Fort Orange Garden Club in Albany and as President of GCA from 1962 until 1965. For her dedication to the organization, she received the Achievement Medal and was the first recipient of the Elizabeth Platt Corning Medal for horticultural excellence at major GCA flower shows, an award endowed in her honor. Betty Corning never missed a GCA meeting until she passed away September 3, 1993.

Betty Corning's contributions to American horticulture and her concern for preserving our natural world were significant. In 1987, Russell Sage College presented her with an honorary Doctor of Humane Letters degree. When accepting the recognition she made the following comments: "I was fortunate in having my eyes opened early to the beauty and wonders of the world which surrounds us. I learned to take time to notice them—to stop, listen to the birds, feel the sunshine, smell the flowers, watch the plants grow, help others, and pat my pets. With these simple precepts, and a love of God, I have found much happiness and am eternally grateful." Gardeners fortunate enough to grow 'Betty Corning' are doubly blessed. The beautiful plant is a garden treasure and perfect reminder of its namesake.

References

Grondahl, Paul. "In the Garden with Betty." *Sunday Times Union* (Albany, New York) September 27, 1992: 1+.

Huxley, Franziska Reed. "Plants: Violet Blue Bells Win the Gold." *Garden Design* May/June, 1992: 82-83.

Poor, Janet Meakin. "A Tribute to Betty Corning." *The Garden Club of America Bulletin* February 1994: 3.

Acknowledgments

Virginia Almand
Joanne Lenden

Photograph courtesy of Bettina Dudley.

JOHN CREECH

John Creech

Abelia x *grandiflora* 'John Creech'

In 21st-century American horticulture, the name of John Lewis Creech is one of the most admired. Born in Woonsocket, Rhode Island, January 17, 1920, Creech's work and accomplishments have been widely recognized, and his curriculum vitae lists numerous distinguished awards. His enormous contributions are further commemorated by two additional legacies: the garden plants that bear his name.

John Creech graduated form the University of Rhode Island with a degree in horticulture in 1941 and then served in World War II from 1941 until 1945 as an officer in the United States Army. Just before leaving for the front lines in 1942, he married Amy Elizabeth Wentzel.

Sent to fight in north Africa, Creech was captured and, from June 1943 until October 1944, was a prisoner of war in Oflag 64 in Schubin, Poland, a German prison camp for officers of the United States ground forces. During the months of his imprisonment, Creech made a most extraordinary contribution to the annals of the war. The Germans turned over a garden plot and greenhouse to the prisoners, and with his newly earned degree and previous training in a family greenhouse in Rhode Island, Creech became manager of the greenhouse at the camp. The Germans allowed him to obtain vegetable seeds and plants from the Red Cross, and with the crops he grew, he supplemented the meager, unpalatable diet provided the prisoners. For this marvelous accomplishment, John Creech was awarded the Bronze Star. He also received the Silver Star for his valor in combat, but, he declares, "my contribution for the Bronze Star [is] far more important as a contribution to my fellow officers."

After the war, Creech returned to school and earned his masters in horticulture in 1947 from the University of Massachusetts. That same year he joined the U.S. Department of Agriculture's Office of Plant Exploration and Introduction at the Plant Industry Station in Beltsville, Maryland. While working, he continued his education in cytogenetics and received his Ph.D. in botany at the University of Maryland in 1953. At the USDA he served as assistant chief of new crops research from 1958 until, in 1968, he was promoted to chief of the agency.

One of the first plants Creech worked with at the Office of Plant Introduction was a collection of abelias. Among them he noted a distinctive dwarf form that he distributed to nurseries. Elizabeth K. Cummins of the Cummins Garden, a nursery in Marlborough, New Jersey, thought the dwarf abelia, which grew to be only 3' tall, was especially useful. Having received it from Creech, she chose to honor him by giving it his name. *Abelia* x *grandiflora* 'John Creech' was introduced in 1953 and is still grown for its unusually small size and its lovely pinkish white flowers.

Creech was associated with Agriculture Research Services between 1955 and 1978 and, during that time, made nine plant exploration trips to Asia, including Japan, China, Taiwan, Nepal, and the USSR. His first expeditions were for economic crops, but later trips were for ornamental exploration. For his meritorious contributions to plant introductions he was awarded the Meyer Medal in 1969.

On an expedition to Siberia in the early 1960s, a sedum with outstanding pink flowers caught Creech's eye. It appeared to be an excellent ground cover for sunny locations and ten years later was distributed by the National Arboretum. André Viette of the Viette Nursery in Fishersville, Virginia, named and included *Sedum* 'John Creech' in his catalogue in the late 1980s.

While Creech was collecting plants in Japan, he learned the language, a skill that was a great benefit to his horticultural work in that country. In 1984, he and a Japanese colleague, Kanane Kato, published a new edition of A *Brocade Pillow: Azaleas of Old Japan*, a seventeenth-century Japanese classic. Creech added an introduction and commentary to Kato's English translation. The Japanese recognized Creech in 1988 with a gold medal and certificate of merit for his contributions to Japanese horticulture, especially for his study of azaleas.

Creech's work for the USDA and his background in plant genetics also allowed him to contribute to the international horticulture community. He was the USDA representative on the Board for Plant Genetic Resources, an international organization located in Rome to benefit developing countries, and also served as the U.S. member of the panel of the Food and Agriculture Organization of the United Nations.

In 1973 John Creech became the director of the National Arboretum in Washington. Under his leadership the Arboretum flourished, and he developed two of its most popular gardens, the National Herb Garden and the National Bonsai and Penjing Museum. The 2.5-acre herb garden comprises a knot garden and theme gardens where visitors enjoy sensory pleasures and informational displays. The National Bonsai and Penjing Museum was the result of Creech's creative diplomacy and experiences in Japan. In 1976 he brought the National Bonsai Collection to the American people as the Bicentennial gift from the Japanese people. It is now the most visited collection at the Arboretum.

After many years of service in the national government, Creech retired in 1980 and moved to North Carolina. Retirement was not a complete change of pace, however, for he became the interim director of the University of North Carolina Arboretum in Asheville and taught biology at the UNC Asheville campus for several years. He also wrote the notes for the 1992 revised edition of Alice Coats's *Garden Shrubs and their Histories*.

Although Creech and his second wife, Elaine Godden Innes, are living in a retirement community, his schedule still includes receiving additional recognition. The Garden Club of America presented him the Gold Medal, and the National Council of State Garden Clubs, the Gold Seal Medal. He has also received the Veitch Memorial Medal from the Royal Horticulture Society, the Liberty Hyde Bailey Medal, and the Award of Merit at the 2000 World Gardens conference. Gardeners are indeed fortunate to be able to plant this handsome abelia and lovely sedum to remind them of John Creech, a giant in American horticulture.

References

Creech, John L. "I Gardened for My Life." *Better Homes and Gardens* October 1946: 150+.

Cunningham, Isabelle Shipley. *Plant Hunter in Asia*. Ames: The Iowa State University Press, 1984.

Who's Who in America. New Providence: Marquis Who's Who, 2000

http://www.ars-grin.gov/ars/Beltsville/na/collectn/bonsai.html

http://www.ars-grin.gov/ars/Beltsville/na/collectn/herb.html

Acknowledgment

John L. Creech

Photograph courtesy of John L. Creech.

47

ROY DAVIDSON

Roy Davidson

Pulmonaria 'Roy Davidson'

Roy Davidson chuckled as he recalled his first plant "discoveries" made when he was a small boy. Each year his parents collected seeds from their garden and kept the packets in the kitchen drawer. Any that spilled from the envelopes and became nameless were given to Roy and his three siblings to plant in their own small garden. Watching their mystery seedlings grow into recognizable plants, Roy remembered his great excitement at "discovering" what they were, particularly when he found his special favorites, the bright sunflowers, towering above all the others. These childhood gardening experiences were only a prologue to the plant discoveries and contributions to American horticulture the young boy from southeastern Washington state would later make.

Born January 15, 1918, Davidson was raised in his mother's family home in the Palouse region of Washington near Colton, eight miles from Pullman. He attended high school in Pullman and graduated in 1935. His parents believed he should attend college, and just one week before the fall session began, his mother acquired a catalogue from Washington State University. Before Roy could enroll, he was instructed to select a major. Among all of the courses offered, only the combined program of ornamental horticulture and landscape design caught his interest. With his major declared, he became a horticulture freshman at Washington State.

For 20 years after he finished college, Roy worked as a floral designer in Bremerton, Washington, then changed careers and became a landscape designer and moved to Seattle. Shortly thereafter, he met Richard Abel, the founder of a small horticulture publishing firm called Timber Press. The two men discovered they shared the same enthusiasm for plants and books, and subsequent conversations led to Abel's asking Roy to write about North American wildflowers.

After several years of work, Roy found the subject of wildflowers so extensive that he abandoned the project. However, it was not to be the end of his book-writing days. A short while later, Abel was searching for someone to continue another terminated project, writing a monograph on the genus *Lewisia*, a native of the western United States. Roy agreed to take it on. He spent many years searching for every species of *lewisia*, often visiting the native habitats in difficult-to-reach places in rugged mountain terrain.

In 1990 Micheal Moshier was hired as the book's illustrator and joined Roy in his pursuit. During the next ten years, the two men concluded the field work and research and in early 2000, Davidson's comprehensive book, *Lewisias* was published. Soon afterward he enjoyed several happy occasions signing his completed work.

Whenever Roy was asked to name his favorite plant, he simply declared, "the one I haven't yet seen." However, there were not many plants Davidson had not seen. He was an authority on lewisias, of course, and extensively studied the western U.S. genera *Iris* and *Penstemon*. Through two plant exploration trips to Japan and many more to the British Isles and Europe, he came to know a wide range of exotics as well. He was always searching for better plants to introduce to American horticulture.

Some examples of Roy Davidson's introductions from his travels include the rose-colored *Hydrangea* 'Pia,' received from a British nursery; *Chamaecyparis pisifera* 'Lime Pie,' purchased at a stall in Shizukoa, Japan; and *Deutzia gracillis* 'Nikko,' from the Nikko Botanic Garden northeast of Tokyo. In acquiring the deutzia, Davidson explained he unknowingly benefited from a Japanese custom: According to his host at Nikko, "a plant admired must be shared." Roy's praise produced a lovely addition for American gardens.

Roy Davidson not only introduced numerous plants, but he shared his experiences through many horticultural publications. Beginning in 1960, more than 65 of his articles appeared in the *Bulletin of the American Rock Garden Society*. As a long-time member of the Northwestern Chapter, he contributed significantly to the society in other ways as well. Besides conducting field trips and sharing his own garden, Davidson organized study weekends and conferences, including the International Rock Plant Conference in Seattle in 1976. The American Rock Garden Society recognized his work by presenting him with prestigious awards, such as the Marcel le Piniec Award in 1972, for "extending and enriching the plant material available to American rock gardeners," and the Marvin Black Award in 1992, for "someone who inspired others to learn and reach their potential in the world of plants."

Roy's generosity also led to his namesake pulmonaria. On a trip to England, he was given a plant of *Pulmonaria longifolia* 'Bertram Anderson' by the outstanding English plantswoman Elizabeth Strangman. Returning to Seattle, Davidson divided and planted his new pulmonaria among other lungworts in his garden. He also promised to give one of the new plants to his gardening friend, Jerry Flintoff. When Flintoff visited Roy to collect his plant, Davidson selected the best of the lot from his row of liners. Although he did not realize it at the time, Davidson had not given Flintoff a clone, but a hybrid seedling that had occurred naturally in his garden. When the lungwort bloomed in Flintoff's garden, he noted at once it differed from 'Bertram Anderson.' The flowers on the new pulmonaria were lighter blue and the spotted, straplike foliage was not quite as long. In Flintoff's words, "I thereupon separated it out and called it several years later after my old friend Roy whom I met in the 1960's and who has done so much for horticulture…in all aspects of plantsmanship." Flintoff's thoughtful gesture immortalized the name of a great American horticulturist.

Roy Davidson's work with iris and lewisia led to two other plants being named for him. Iris 'Roy Davidson' is a beardless yellow-flowered hybrid with brown veins and signals, probably a cross between I. *pseudacorus* and I. *foetidissima*. The other namesake is *Lewisia cotyledon* var. *fimbriata* 'Roy Davidson,' a white-flowering form collected by Steven Darington from the rock faces of the Trinity River Canyon in California.

Roy Davidson died November 28, 2000. A memorial service was held at his beautiful garden in Bellevue, Washington, in the spring of 2001. For his friend's obituary in the *Bulletin of the American Rock Garden Society*, Micheal Moshier, the artist of the exquisite botanical paintings for Lewisias, wrote the following, "Traveling and exploring with Roy was like having a walking, talking encyclopedia and world atlas in hand at once as he related his exhaustive knowledge of plants, their natural history, and the geographical background accompanying their habitat.… Many of us will long cherish our memories of him hiking through the mountains he loved so dearly, walking stick in hand, his keen eyes scrutinizing the alpine landscape about him, not missing one detail nor leaving one stone unturned."

References

Bender, Pat. "Marvin Black Award, B. LeRoy Davidson." *Bulletin of the American Rock Garden Society* Fall 1992: 299.

Brickell, Christopher and, Judith D. Zuk, Editors in Chief. *The American Horticultural Society A–Z Encyclopedia of Garden Plants*. New York: DK Publishing, Inc., 1997.

Davidson, B. LeRoy. *Lewisias*. Portland: Timber Press, 2000.

Davidson, B. LeRoy. "Discoveries and Introductions." UW *Arboretum Bulletin*. Winter 1980 : 26-31.

Flook, Marnie. A *History of the American Rock Garden Society*, 1934–1995. Manhattan: AgPress, 1997.

Acknowledgments

Tony Avent

Roy Davidson

Valerie Easton

Jerry John Flintoff

Ferdinand Minici

Micheal Moshier

Photograph by George Waters courtesy of Ferdinand Minici.

VINCE AND
BARBARA DOOLEY

Vince and Barbara Dooley

Hydrangea macrophylla 'Dooley'

Those who have heard of Vince Dooley do not usually associate his name with anything other than athletics, specifically football. His athletic credentials are impressive: He was an all-star football and basketball player at Auburn University. His success in athletics continued when he became the extremely successful football coach at the University of Georgia from 1964 to 1988, and when he assumed his present position as the university's Athletic Director. His awards and credits are too numerous to list, but a few highlights include guiding his teams to 20 bowl games, being inducted into the College Football Hall of Fame, and receiving the prestigious Amos Alonzo Stagg Award for lifetime contributions to the sport of football.

However, to appreciate the man, one needs to peel away the cloak of athletics and view his other accomplishments. His contributions to the community are exhaustive. Dooley's work with the Heart Fund, Multiple Sclerosis, Juvenile Diabetes, Boy Scouts and the Salvation Army are legendary, and for the last 28 years, he has chaired the Georgia Easter Seal Society. In 1990, in honor of his many years of work for that cause, a new Easter Seals facility was built in Atlanta and named for him. All this came from a man most people know only as a football coach.

Dooley is a man who thrives on learning. He will tell you that "the great thing about a University is that a person can satisfy a quest for anything" and a quest for learning is what best defines Dooley. He will show up in undergraduate courses on such varied subjects as art appreciation, civil war history, and horticulture. When Dooley walks into a class, you might expect that students would treat him like a celebrity; however, he is accepted simply as another student who sits in a chair, asks questions where appropriate, and takes notes like the rest.

At the Dooley family home, the garden was always neat and well kept but, in the 1990's, Vince's interest in gardening awoke when he took some horticulture classes from Professors Dirr and Armitage. The garden was quickly transformed into a repository for many of Dirr's favorite plants. Today, the property is a mini-arboretum, with an outstanding collection of trees, shrubs, and water features. People admire it from the street and those fortunate enough to visit soon appreciate Dooley's love of trees. And the garden keeps getting bigger. Each year Dooley creeps a little farther onto his neighbor's property. Give him time, someone has said, and he will have the entire neighborhood planted with trees.

The Dooley garden has been featured in publications around the Southeast and nationally on such programs as Victory Garden, Rebecca's Garden, and Home and Garden TV. Vince will talk about plants to anyone who will listen, and, his wife, Barbara, has long ago given up expecting more than another Japanese maple for her birthday. Hoping, yes, expecting, no. Like their garden, the Dooley family continues to grow, and presently includes four children and nine grandchildren, and counting.

When asked about the genesis of his gardening passion, he credits the guru of woody plants, Michael Dirr, with flaming the fires of horticulture. In 1999, Dooley and Dirr led a concerted effort to recognize the outstanding tree plantings on the campus of the University of Georgia, and with the help of faculty and campus planners, the campus was designated an arboretum. Hundreds of trees have been labeled and booklets for self guided-tours were created.

The Dooley/Dirr friendship must also be credited for the introduction of the fine blue mophead hydrangea 'Dooley'. In 1968, Barbara acquired the original bush from an Athens nursery owned by George Upchurch when it was going out of business. She took it home and stuck it in a bed by the house. For more than 25 years, it simply appeared to be one more blue hydrangea dotting the late spring landscapes in the Athens area.

In 1996, however, when a late freeze killed the flower buds of most of the hydrangeas in the area, the horticulturist in Dooley noted that this particular hydrangea seemed unaffected. When another late freeze occurred in 1998, with similar devastating results to other hydrangeas, Dirr also took serious notice of this seemingly indestructible plant. Scientific tests have confirmed the plant's cold hardiness, which can be attributed to the large number of lateral flower buds it produces, making possible an abundance of flowers, even if the terminal buds are frozen.

Not only is its cold hardiness noteworthy, but the shrub's color, vigor, and ease of propagation make it a favorite of nursery people and gardeners alike. Dirr named the plant *Hydrangea macrophylla* 'Dooley', and it first appeared in the Spring Meadow Nursery catalog in 1998.

Vince Dooley was born in Mobile Alabama in 1932, and although he found great success as an athlete as a young man, his courtship and marriage to Barbara Meshad in 1960 was the smartest thing he ever did. Barbara is very much her own woman, and her success rests comfortably alongside her husband's. She hosts a regular radio show and is in constant demand as a speaker around the country. Together, they make an unbeatable pair, each complementing the other. As a team, they are far stronger than their individual parts.

The Dooley hydrangea has given gardeners a terrific plant, but more importantly, it celebrates an outstanding renaissance man and his wife. Vince and Barbara need no more fame or glory for they have those in abundance, but their legacy will continue to grow whenever a Dooley hydrangea is planted.

Acknowledgments
Barbara and Vince Dooley
Becky Stevens

Photo courtesy of Vince Dooley.

ECO-GARDENS

Don Jacobs

Lysimachia congestiflora 'Eco Dark Satin'

D on Jacobs, an ecologist by training, retired from teaching at the University of Georgia in 1956, and purchased six acres of land near Atlanta which he named Eco-Gardens, an appellation that inherently states his mission. The garden's introductions of distinctive plants coupled with its contributions to the protection of endangered plant species, Eco-Gardens is widely recognized in the world of horticulture.

Jacobs's unusual plant collections include both native and Asian species suitable for the southeastern climate. He selects and tests potential new offerings, and after successful propagation, he distributes his limited supply to collectors, botanical gardens, and commercial nurseries.

"Eco" always becomes a by-line to each new introduction. Some examples of the several hundred Eco plants are *Lysimachia congestiflora* 'Eco Dark Satin'; *Trillium cuneatum* 'Eco Dappled Lemon,' 'Eco Green Phantom,' and 'Eco Marbled Lime'; *Pachysandra procumbens* 'Eco Picture Leaf'; *Chrysogonum* 'Eco Lacquered Spider'; *Phlox nivalis* 'Eco Flirtie Eyes'; and *Heuchera* 'Eco Magnififolia.'

Interest in gardening and ecology came naturally to Don Jacobs. He was born in the North Dakota prairie town of Hebron and fondly remembers the fragrance of beautiful petunias and stocks filling his grandmother's garden. While he was still a young boy, the Jacobs family moved to Arlington, Minnesota, where he attended grade school and spent endless hours exploring the natural landscape of the Big Woods.

In 1928, when he was nine years old, the family moved to Minneapolis, but even in the city, Jacobs maintained his love of nature. He worked as a "nature" counselor in the summers and enjoyed sharing experiences of the great outdoors with young campers. After graduating from high school, he remained in Minneapolis for college and graduate school and received a Ph.D. degree in Ecology from the University of Minnesota in 1946.

Jacobs's first job took him to Mankato State University in Minnesota. Recruited to replace the chairman of the biology department who had died midterm, he found himself teaching courses in genetics, bacteriology, ornithology, plant geography, and field ecology. After a year and a half of this intense classroom schedule, Don heard about a position in the Botany Department at the University of Georgia. Persuaded the south was a viable frontier for research in field ecology, Jacobs moved to Athens and joined the faculty in 1948. He quickly became enamored with the southeast and remained at Georgia until he retired.

He did not immediately start his nursery. In fact, his love for animals was the incentive for his next career, a pet supply business centered around fish and aquatic plants, an interest he had begun to develop in Minneapolis. Jacobs became well known in the world of aquarium culture and was a contributing editor to *Aquarium Magazine*. He also made an important discovery of an aquarium protozoan parasite and published the book *Knowing Your Aquarium Plants*. Reptiles were another interest, and he contributed numerous articles to the *Journal of the American Herpetology Society*. However, in the 1970s, after two decades of selling pet supplies, he sold that business and turned all of his attention to his garden and plants.

Always an avid gardener, Jacobs moved naturally into the development of Eco-Gardens and paid particular attention to the connection between American and Asian plants as they related to the southeastern climate To further his knowledge about those plants, he made three collecting trips to Asia in the 1980s. China, Japan, Eastern Mongolia, Thailand, Singapore, and Taiwan were his exotic destinations. In 1983, he was on Mt. Emei in Sechuan, China, and noticed a free-flowering prostrate loose-strife (*Lysimachia congestiflora*) which he brought back to Georgia. The plant did not survive the trip, but some of its seeds did. Of the seven resulting seedlings, one produced larger, showier flowers than the others. However, it was the noticeable satiny sheen of the foliage that caught Jacobs's eye and led him to name the new plant *Lysicmachia congestiflora* 'Eco Dark Satin.' It has become one of his most popular introductions.

Jacobs also traveled throughout North America to observe native flora, particularly trilliums. During the long winters while he was growing up, he always looked forward to the emergence of those harbingers of spring. Admiration for the genus, led Don and his son, Rob, to publish *American Treasures: Trilliums in the Woodland Gardens*, in 1997. The father and son are passionate about conservation of woodlands and believe trilliums arc "inseparably intertwined with concepts of conservation…." The Printing Industry Association of the South honored their book with its Award of Excellence in 1998.

Another plant discovery resulted from a trip to Weaverville, North Carolina, the hometown of Don's daughter-in-law, Maria. Don found large numbers of *Heuchera americana* growing in the nearby woods, one with an extremely showy leaf. He took it to his nursery, and after building up a population, he introduced it as *Heuchera* 'Eco Magnififolia.' It remains one of Eco-Gardens best-known plants.

Within the framework of ecology, Don Jacobs is an expert about many subjects. His passion for exploring the relationship between plant and animal life has led him to share an enormous amount of beneficial information. Horticulturists and gardeners have enjoyed an abundance of exciting new plants from Eco-Gardens. Without question, the term "Eco" is a symbol of the exceptional work of Don Jacobs.

And, there is now an "Eco-Gardens II," a picturesque garden north of Atlanta, created by Rob and Maria. In a lovely wooded brookside ravine, they concentrate on growing and protecting American native plants. There is no doubt Rob is the offspring of his ecologist parent, Don Jacobs.

References

Jacobs, Don. "*Lysimachia congestiflora*, Another of Mt. Emei's Treasures." *Bulletin of the American Rock Garden Society* Summer 1985:135-138.

Jacobs, Don. "From China with Concern." *Bulletin of the American Rock Garden Society* Spring 1993:136-144.

Jacobs, Don and Jacobs, Rob. *American Treasures, Trilliums in the Woodland Garden*. Decatur: Eco-Gardens, 1997.

Acknowledgment

Don Jacobs

Photograph courtesy of Don Jacobs.

KATIE FERGUSON

Katie Ferguson

Ruellia britonniana 'Katie'

Mexican petunias, botanically known as *Ruellia*, are annuals in most of the country; however, they are not petunias at all, even though the plant's tubular shaped flowers often remind gardeners of the popular old fashioned annuals. As their common name also suggests, the plants thrive in hot climates. They have become quite popular in the southern United States, and gardeners elsewhere have also discovered the charm and functionality of this fine group of plants. One that is especially appealing is the dwarf form named 'Katie.'

Ruellia 'Katie' made its debut in Texas in 1982 at the Lowrey Nursery in Conroe. A natural hybrid reaching no more than a foot in height, 'Katie' arose from a seedling as a dwarf form of *Ruellia britonniana*, which commonly grows 3'-5' tall. The plant was named by Texas nurseryman Lynn Lowrey for Katharine (Katie) Fulcher Ferguson, the friend and colleague who had purchased his nursery only a few months before the plant was discovered.

Katie Fulcher grew up in the west Texas town of Odessa, where she was born January 15, 1942. Her father was a surgeon, and her mother, a former dancer, was an avid reader and collector of books, and both were well known and respected in their community. After elementary school, Katie attended prep school in San Antonio, then graduated with a degree in art from Mt. Holyoke College in 1964. She lived in Italy for a year after college, immersing herself in the country's art, culture, and language.

Upon her return to the United States, Katie was hired as a buyer of women's clothing in Houston and New York for Foley's department store. The tall, beautiful, elegant woman was a natural in the world of fashion. Later she became the manager for designer Roberta de Camerino's boutique in Houston.

Outside her career, Katie's talents, personality, and interests were further demonstrated. She created interior designs and flower arrangements that became features in numerous magazine stories; and, in her community she founded a writing program for young patients at M. D. Anderson Hospital in Houston. Her energy knew no bounds.

After her marriage and the birth of her daughter, Tito, in 1975, Ferguson made a major career change. While landscaping her home in Houston with the help of nurseryman Lynn Lowrey, she discovered a passion for the world of plants and gardening. Ferguson and Lowrey developed a great friendship. With Katie's sense of color and love of perennials and Lynn's knowledge of woodies, especially their use in natural landscapes, the two made a winning team. Ferguson spent a great deal of time working at Lowrey's nursery, and when he decided to sell his business in August 1982, she purchased it.

Described by her friends as flamboyant, vivacious, and full of life and fun, Katie made her everyday fashion of gypsy-like costumes with bright shawls and flowing skirts her trademark. Nurseryman Tommy Dodd remembers meeting Katie while attending plant conventions in Texas. After the meetings they would pile into Katie's old Chevy station wagon, which, he says, she "drove like an Italian while listening to anything from Mozart to Gordon Lightfoot," and head for some out-of-the-way Mexican restaurant where Katie, speaking fluent Spanish, would place their order. Her new life in the world of plants brought her great pleasure and a new circle of friends.

Not long after Ferguson purchased Lowrey's nursery, two of the employees, Herbert Durand and Noland Guillot, discovered the dwarf ruellia and reported it to Lowrey. After being assured it was a worthy garden plant, Lowrey named it 'Katie.' The honoree was thrilled to have a plant named for her, and she enjoyed sharing it with her friends. Fellow members of Houston's River Oaks Garden Club remember the meeting when she happily told them about her namesake plant and gave them each a sample. Lowrey Nursery introduced and successfully promoted the new plant discovery, and *Ruellia britonniana* 'Katie' became a hit.

In 1990, Katie Ferguson was diagnosed with a recurrence of breast cancer. Seeking to fight her disease and to explore possible cures, she learned of studies using the Tree of Joy, *Campatheca acuminata*, a plant she was growing at her nursery. She participated in a study and was given one of the first oral dosages of the experimental cure. However, the cancer took her life on January 7, 1993, just eight days before her fifty-first birthday.

Traveling varied paths during her lifetime, Katie touched the lives of many people and is remembered with affection and respect. It is indeed fortunate that Lynn Lowrey immortalized this extraordinary woman by giving her name to a lovely and exciting plant.

Ferguson's friend Tommy Dodd also recently introduced a rhododendron in her name. *Rhododendron* x *oblongifolium* 'Katie Ferguson,' one of four hybrids resulting from crosses made in 1980 by his father, Tom Dodd. With bright, blazing pink flowers, *R.* 'Katie Ferguson' is an apt addition to the legacy of this delightful, colorful plantswoman.

Reference

Pickens, Mary Anne. "Lynn R. Lowrey, Plantsman." *Magnolia, Bulletin of the Southern Garden History Society* Summer 1999: 1, 3-8.

Acknowledgments

Patsy Lowrey Anderson
Tommy Dodd
Marion Drummond
Tito Ferguson
CeCe Fowler
Greg Grant
Mary Ann Pickens
Ted Pinson
William Welch

Photograph courtesy of Marion Drummond.

HENRY AND SALLY FULLER

Henry and Sally Fuller

Phlox divaricata 'Fuller's White'

Henry and Sally Fuller spent nearly 40 years creating out-standing gardens at their homes in Easton, Connecticut. Most gardeners have a difficult time making a single garden, but, as the result of a fire destroying their first home, the Fullers developed their second garden only a few miles from their first. At both sites, their rock gardens and plant displays were leg-endary, and they gained widespread recognition as exceptional gardeners and knowledgeable plantspeople.

The light blue–flowered native woodland *phlox divaricata* was a plant much beloved by both Henry and Sally. Sally had said it was her favorite for drift planting because she loved to see the delicate stems sway in the wind. While both of them enjoyed the blue flowers, it was their dream to discover a white-flowered form. In the 1950s they purchased a robust strain of woodland phlox from Vermont nurseryman Fred Abbey, and, although they did not know it at the time, they were on their way to achieving their goal.

They planted the new plants in a large bed they fondly called their "Jewel Box." However, for many years, all of their "jewels" remained blue. Finally, one spring morning in the early 1960s, Sally spied a pure white flower amidst the sea of blue. Quickly she fetched her husband, but when they returned, the white bloom was no longer there! Henry later wrote, "Some devil in rabbit's clothing must have eaten it…," a devil referred to by Sally as "…a real Devil in the form of a mind-reading rabbit who watched me from dark evil passages and rushed out and ate ravenously when he saw my face light up." After frantic searching, however, they found a plant with a "nibbled-off" stem. With great anticipation they potted up the flowerless plant and were rewarded the following spring. Henry and Sally Fuller had at last found their white-flowered treasure.

When Henry reported the discovery, he touted the new white phlox as a strong grower, easily propagated by cuttings and divisions. In addition, it is content to be planted almost anywhere in the garden, as long as it is shaded from the summer sun. When 'Fuller's White' is compared to the species, it is more dwarf and so completely covered with clear, white flowers in the spring that it looks like a snowbank.

One of the Fullers' closest friends, H. Lincoln Foster, spoke at the 1971 American Rock Garden Society meeting in Atlantic City, where he first referred to their phlox as 'Fuller's White.' The same year Roy Elliott, president of the Alpine Garden Society of Great Britain, pronounced it to be "one of the best of ten new plants given to the horticultural world in a ten-year period." Since that time, the Fullers' plant has been admired in gardens throughout the world, even appearing in Australia and New Zealand.

With a career designed to provide maximum time to enjoy his avocation of gardening, Henry was one of the best College Division salesmen for the publishing firm of Houghton Mifflin, a job that kept him busiest during the school year months. When summer vacation time arrived, he was free to spend more time developing gardens and nurturing plants. Henry's enormous passion for gardening might have been an inherited trait. His middle name came from his mother's family, the Reasoners, who distinguished themselves in Florida horticulture. A Manatee County pioneer family, they founded Royal Palm Nurseries in Oneco in 1881, a mail-order nursery specializing in exotic, especially tropical, plants. They introduced bougainvillea, avocado, lychee, mango, and the first pink grapefruit to their clients. Henry grew up surrounded by the family's love for plants.

Henry Reasoner Fuller was one of three boys and two girls and was next to the youngest in age. He was born July 4, 1902, and grew up in Bradenton, Florida, where he graduated in 1921 from Manatee County High School. He received a degree in English literature from the University of North Carolina in 1926, and afterward went to Europe with the idea of becoming a foreign missionary. A year later, he dismissed that idea and returned to Chapel Hill.

There he met Selma (Sally) McComas, a graduate student, and they were married in 1929. Henry worked for a year at the University of North Carolina Press before Houghton Mifflin hired him and sent him to Louisville, Kentucky. In 1937, Houghton Mifflin moved Henry to New York City to work in the New England region of their college textbook division. The Fullers moved to Easton, Connecticut in 1940 and began to construct their first garden, a labor of love they enjoyed so much, they did it a second time.

Henry and Sally had many interests and many friends. Henry's job and avocation introduced him to people everywhere, and all who knew him remember an outgoing and warm-hearted man. Sally, who grew up in Kentucky, was a wonderful cook and a great storyteller in the Southern tradition. The couple were marvelous hosts to a broad range of people who represented many concerns and curiosities. One of Henry's main causes was the Neo-conservative political movement that opposed the social restrictions of Communism. But gardening and plants consumed most of Henry and Sally's free time, and even before Henry retired in 1969, their achievements and contributions to gardening were significant.

There is no doubt the Fullers were avid rock gardeners: One of their Easton neighbors good-naturedly recalls being told by Henry that she should turn her entire lawn into a rock garden! They were devoted to American Rock Garden Society which they joined around 1950. They found its related international branches also helpful for research, information, and plant distribution, and through this link, maintained correspondence with a number of members in other countries. In 1968, Henry helped to found the Rock Garden Society's Connecticut Chapter and was its first Chairman. He also chaired the ARGS Seed Exchange from 1969 to 1971 and served as a national director. For his many contributions, including the discovery of *Phlox divaricata* 'Fuller's White,' the ARGS awarded him its most prestigious prize, the Award of Merit, in 1977.

Toward the end of his gardening career, Henry became enamored with native azaleas and joined the American Rhododendron Society. With friends and fellow rhododendron enthusiasts, he traveled in the Blue Ridge Mountains and was captivated by the magnificent display of native azaleas. The Fuller garden became home to a fine collection of these plants, and when Henry finally left his garden, he was thrilled to have the Tyler Arboretum in Lima, Pennsylvania, accept his plants as part of their native azalea collection.

Sally Fuller became ill in the mid 1970s and died in 1977. Henry continued to live at their home on Sherwood Road in Easton until 1980, when, after almost completely losing his sight, he returned to Bradenton and lived in a retirement home. During those final years, he maintained his intellectual curiosity and actively filled his days with friends and family until he died on January 3, 2001, at the age of 98.

Henry and Sally Fuller were an outstanding gardening couple who discovered a lovely plant, and it is fitting that the white-flowered woodland phlox is named for them. Gardeners who grow *Phlox divaricata* 'Fuller's White' can fondly remember this remarkable pair who inspired their contemporaries in so many ways.

References

Fuller, Henry. "Phlox divaricata 'Fuller's White.'" *Bulletin of the American Rock Garden Society* Winter 1978: 19.

Merillat, Catherine. "Prize Plants Nurtured in Easton Garden by Couple Who are Dedicated to Flowers." *Bridgeport Sunday Post* June 3, 1973: C-1.

Page, Virginia. "Native Enjoys Music World." *The Bradenton Herald* December 25, 1990: 13.

http://www.royalpalmnurseries.com/press.htm

Acknowledgments

Frank Cabot
Marnie Flook
Doris Giles
Rich Lee
Richard Redfield

Photograph courtesy of Rich Lee.

FRED GALLE

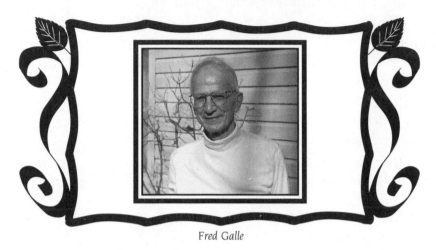

Fred Galle

Rhododendron 'Galle's Choice'

To many people the name Fred Galle (pronounced as in galley of a ship) is synonymous with azaleas, an appropriate association for the man who, in 1985, published *Azaleas*, the 486-page definitive reference. Therefore, it is also fitting that he selected a deciduous azalea to bear his name. *Rhododendron* 'Galle's Choice' resulted from a cross he made of the flame azalea, *Rhododendron calendulaceum*, and the Alabama azalea, *Rhododendron alabamense*, to produce an interspecific hybrid with a delightful fragrance and stunning light yellow flowers, further enhanced by large, wavy lobes edged in a tinge of pink. Struck by its beauty, Galle proclaimed this one his favorite of all the many azalea crosses he made.

Galle is also known for his long association with Callaway Gardens in Pine Mountain, Georgia, a magnificent public garden noted for its woodlands and spectacular springtime azalea display. Galle was its Director of Horticulture for 27 years and then served 3 years as Curator of the gardens. During that time he promoted the introduction of several plants associated with Callaway such as a ginger (*Asarum shuttleworthii* 'Callaway'), a crab apple (*Malus* 'Callaway'), and a summersweet clethra (*Clethra alnifolia* 'Hummingbird').

Although this remarkable horticulturist is most closely associated with the South, Galle was born and raised in Dayton, Ohio. The beautiful flowers in his father's rock garden are his first gardening memories, but boyhood activities such as Scouting, hiking, and camping, instilled him with a passion for native plants. After graduating from high school in 1937, Galle spent two years working at odd jobs before entering Michigan State University to study forestry. After one year there, he transferred to Ohio State University, changed his course of study to horticulture, and graduated in 1943.

One summer during his school years, Fred worked as a lifeguard at a pool in Dayton, where he met his future wife, Betty. Remaining friends while they continued their educations, they courted during their service in World War II: Betty as a nurse and Fred, in the Army. They married in Europe after the war and returned to Ohio where Galle obtained his master's degree in horticulture from Ohio State in 1946. His first teaching position was in Knoxville, where he joined the faculty of the University of Tennessee to start a Department for Ornamental Horticulture.

After five years in Knoxville, Galle returned to Ohio State to teach, do research and, he hoped, finish the doctorate he had begun at Tennessee. His Ph.D. pursuit, however, came to a memorable and incomplete conclusion.

Galle told the amazing story of how he and Ben Pace, a fellow faculty member and later a co-worker at Callaway Gardens, were collecting seeds on Gregory Bald in the Smoky Mountains where Galle was studying a colony of deciduous azaleas. The two men were carrying backpacks, and each pack had quite different contents. Pace's contained their food, but Galle's was much more valuable: it held his notebook filled with seven years of research data collected for his dissertation. One morning during their trip, Pace and Galle left their camp for a trek up the Bald to view the sunrise. During their absence, a curious bear discovered their unattended packs. For some reason the bear took more of a liking to the scholar's cache than to the pack with food, and the hairy intruder escaped with Galle's work. Galle's notebook was never found and the loss prompted him, with much regret, to abandon his research. However, his years in academia had established him as a significant plantsman, particularly in native azaleas, and his expertise and recognition brought his name to the attention of Cason Callaway, the founder of Callaway Gardens.

In 1930, Cason and Virginia Hand Callaway had purchased a large tract of land in Hamilton, Georgia, a small town adjacent to Pine Mountain. They were making plans to transform the property from abandoned cotton fields, into lakes and gardens featuring native plants, especially native azaleas, a plant permanently endeared to them ever since they discovered the summer-blooming plumleaf azalea while on a picnic in the area. Because *Rhododendron prunifolium*, the crimson-flowered plumleaf, is indigenous only within a 100-mile radius of Callaway Gardens, the Callaways had found the perfect plant to become the symbol of their enterprise: The plumleaf azalea is featured today as the garden's logo. In Fred Galle, the Callaways now found the perfect plantsman to make their garden of native plants into a reality.

When Fred received the offer to direct the horticulture program at Callaway Gardens, he and Betty left an unusually cold winter in Ohio for their first visit to Callaway. They could hardly believe the wonderful climate they found in Georgia, and they had no trouble making their decision. Galle accepted the position, and, in 1953, they happily moved to Hamilton with their two young children, Phil and Peggy.

During Galle's years at Callaway, he oversaw tremendous development in the gardens and, finally, the fruition of the Callaways' plan for an enjoyable and educational public garden. In the beginning, Galle and Virginia Callaway rescued many plants from the wild and transplanted them to the garden, especially the many native azaleas that dotted the landscape. As the gardens' needs grew, Galle upgraded and increased the number of greenhouses, began research programs, and consulted with many horticulturists. He also traveled to the British Isles and to Japan for additional plant acquisitions. Through Galle's propagation and collecting efforts, the gardens' plant population and diversity increased significantly.

Another important part of the Galle legacy at Callaway is the prestigious student intern program in horticulture. One of these summer interns was a student from Ohio State, Rick Feist, who was responsible for naming *Clethra alnifolia* 'Hummingbird.' The original plant was collected by Galle in Tolbert County, Georgia, about 40 miles from Callaway. Galle took the plant back to the gardens, grew it for a year in a holding bed, then placed it at the edge of Hummingbird Lake for further study. It resided there for many years until Feist observed its slow-growing, compact, dwarf habit and suggested that it deserved recognition. He insured its fame by christening it 'Hummingbird'.

Clethra alnfolia 'Hummingbird' was registered in 1991 and received the Gold Medal Plant Award from the Pennsylvania Horticulture Society in 1994. With its white summer flowers, compact habit, and sweet clethra fragrance, it has become a hugely popular garden plant.

Because of Galle's reputation, many people interested in native plants sought his expertise. One of these was Frank Bloodworth of Decatur, Georgia, who gardened with native plants collected throughout the Southeast. When Bloodworth died, his daughter invited Galle to return to her father's garden to collect any plants he felt would be useful. Among others, he selected a large clump of native ginger, distinguished by small, beautifully mottled leaves. Galle noted later that, although Bloodworth had kept excellent records in most cases, he had failed to record where he had found this ginger. Therefore, when Galle took the plant back to Callaway Gardens, he decided to name it for the native plant garden with which he himself was so closely associated. Thus, *Asarum shuttleworthii* 'Callaway' came to be.

Another plant associated with Galle originated in an order of

73

ten crabapples from a nursery in Ohio. Galle discovered that one seedling was not true to name; nonetheless, because it seemed to be a particularly good-looking plant, he showed it to nursery friends from Tennessee, Hoskins Shadow and Hubert Nicholson. They were sufficiently impressed by the tree and decided to market it, calling it *Malus* 'Callaway'. After its display of handsome light pink spring flowers, *M.* 'Callaway' produces showy medium-sized fruits in the fall. 'Callaway' is, according to Galle, one of the best crabapples for southern gardens.

Although it has no cultivar name, *Silene polypetala*, fringed campion, listed as an endangered plant in Georgia, is now available to gardeners partly because of Fred Galle's enthusiasm for native plants. He first discovered the plant as a specimen in the herbarium at the University of Georgia. Noting in the documentation that the original plant had been growing on the banks of the Flint River in the middle part of the state, Galle decided to find the plant. After many trips, he finally discovered it on the riverbank about 40 miles east of Pine Mountain. He took the plant back to Callaway Gardens where he propagated it from cuttings. He distributed it to nurseries, and today it is possible for plant lovers to enjoy the delicate beauty of the pale pink, deeply fringed flowers in their own gardens.

Fred Galle retired from Callaway in 1983, and he and Betty lived in Hamilton until 1997 when they moved to Illinois. That year he published another monumental book, *Hollies, the Genus Ilex*, describing more than 800 species.

For his immense contributions to horticulture, Galle received many recognitions, among them, the Liberty Hyde Bailey Medal from the American Horticulture Society, the Gold Medal from the American Rhododendron Society, and the Arthur Hoyt Scott Garden and Horticulture Award from Swarthmore College.

Fred Galle died in 1998, but the many named plants he provided allow every gardener the opportunity to be reminded of this exceptional American horticulturist.

Reference

Callaway, Howard H. *The Story of a Man and a Garden, Cason Callaway and Callaway Gardens*. New York: The Newcomen Society of North America, 1965.

Acknowledgment

Fred and Betty Galle

Photograph by Linda Copeland.

GARDENVIEW HORTICULTURAL PARK

Henry Ross

Monarda 'Gardenview Scarlet'

Henry Ross is an impassioned gardener with definite opinions about his chosen occupation. It is difficult to tell his story and that of the plants he has named without becoming inspired by his thoughts and arguments for improving the gardening atmosphere in the United States.

To illustrate his convictions, Ross single-handedly created Gardenview Horticultural Park, his "oasis of beauty," an outstanding 16-acre garden in Strongsville, Ohio, just southwest of Cleveland. His development of Gardenview is almost inconceivable, especially because for more than 40 years he worked alone.

Henry Ross began gardening with his mother at their home in Cleveland when he was eight years old. He remembers mischievously picking bouquets from her large circle of peonies and sweet Williams and looks back upon those happy boyhood experiences as the beginning of his dream of one day creating his own garden. In 1949, during a drive home from Columbus, where he was a student at Ohio State University, he passed through Strongsville and saw a "for sale" sign. He looked over the property and even though it was covered with snow, decided to borrow the money to purchase what would become his future garden. Although it is completely surrounded by development today, Gardenview Horticultural Park remains viable and always will be, if Henry has his way.

In the spring, when the snow melted, Ross discovered that he possessed a swamp of blue clay. There was no doubt that if he was going to succeed at making a garden, he would be engaged in a never-ending labor of love. His first attempt to amend the clay was a disaster. He added tons of sand, but because it was from a foundry, it was black with oil. After correcting this first mistake, he began adding horse manure from local riding stables until all of Gardenview sat on up to three feet of water-repellent compost. Initially, water was plentiful, and it was not difficult to give his garden the moisture required, but urban sprawl around Gardenview cut off his natural supply and water became a concern. Ross met the challenges, however, and created a garden which is a must-see destination for all gardeners. He worked at the monumental project alone until 1994, when a young man named Mark LaRosa joined him as his Assistant Director.

Gardenview consists of two main areas, a 6-acre area of irregularly shaped gardens separated by meandering paths, and a 10-acre arboretum containing more than 2,500 unusual trees and shrubs. Ross began his garden by planting trees. His favorites were flowering crabapples, but he insists the ones available when he started were "crummy." Consequently, he began seeking out crabapples for Gardenview, and eventually collected over 500 varieties, including some he originated. In the 1950s, three of these became his first patents, *Malus* 'White Cascade,' *M.* 'Coral Cascade,' and, *M.* 'Coralburst,' the last being his most exceptional: a polyploid with small, boxwood-like leaves and one-inch, roselike double white flowers that unfold from bright coral-pink buds. After planting hundreds of trees, this insatiable horticulturist sought and found countless plants to install throughout the entire garden. Ross' extensive collection became the source of many Gardenview introductions.

Monarda 'Gardenview Scarlet' is one of the best known. Introduced in the early 1970s, Ross discovered it among self-sown seedlings, probably from *Monarda* 'Adam', and propagated it for Gardenview. The raves it drew from visitors caused Ross to distribute it to nurserymen. Not only did the 3'-5' tall plant have a lovely flower, it showed virtually no mildew at Gardenview, Ross did not choose the name, and in his typically adamant style, he quibbles with the "scarlet" part of the title. He claims Gardenview Red would be a more accurate representation of the flower's rose-red color.

Before Ross explains about his *Ajuga* 'Arctic Fox,' he will tell you about his great affection for variegated foliage, and often an instruction on variegation patterns will ensue. He is well-versed in the different forms of variegation and the difficulties inherent in propagating variegated plants. Because it originated as an almost totally white leaf sport discovered on a green ajuga, 'Artic Fox' illustrates the difficulties. But, Ross succeeded in cloning his discovery, and the frosty white–leaved ajuga with its distinctive dark green edge and silver-stroked midrib became available in 1980. The plant's name, however, resulted from an incorrect assumption by its breeder. According to Ross, he thought an arctic fox was white, but the animal is actually gray. Nonetheless, the white foliage of this 'Arctic Fox' makes a splendid background for its purple flowers.

Gold-colored leaves also have great appeal to Ross. His *Hosta* 'Solar Flare' is testimony to that fascination. Its enormous leaves emerge chartreuse in the spring, but as the summer progresses, their veins become Kelly green and contrast wonderfully with the golden green color.

Henry still surprises people with new additions to the introductions from Gardenview. Visitors there will see not only all of these, but also a large number of other rare and unusual specimens such as a large colony of variegated brunnera, *Brunnera macrophylla* 'Variegata.' The purpose of Gardenview, as stated in its brochure, is to provide enjoyment to visitors, to demonstrate the art of English Cottage Gardening and of traditional perennial borders, and to give an opportunity…to adapt these ideas and planting combinations to their own gardens." According to Ross, "Gardenview is not intended for the general public, but it exists for those people who garden and love plants"; and the pleasures are endless.

With strong ideas about horticulture, Ross enjoys espousing his causes and takes every opportunity to proselytize. He is quick to point out that *Monarda* 'Gardenview Scarlet' is a clone, not a cultivar, for it is vegetatively reproduced. He has written extensively about this subject and many others and often provokes thoughtful and needed dialog about horticulture topics.

This unique individual and creator of Gardenview Horticultural Park, hopes that his garden will continue long after he can care for it. He made it a gift to the public as a tax-exempt corporation, and he and Mark continue to raise funds to endow its maintenance for the future. Henry Ross, his work at Gardenview, and his many plant introductions have forever enhanced American horticulture.

Reference

Fischer, Thomas. "Gardenview, A Plantsman's Paradise." *Horticulture* May 1994: 42-48.

Ross, Henry. "A plea for real gardens and real gardening." *Ameican Nurseryman* October 1, 1987: 65-66.

Acknowledgment
Henry Ross

Photograph by Linda Copeland.

AZILDA GERBING

Azilda Gerbing

Rhododendron 'Mrs. G. G. Gerbing'

Gustav George Gerbing (Gus) harvested oysters off the Fernandina, Florida, coast on 490 acres of leased oyster beds he had inherited from his father. As he made deliveries to the surrounding areas an interesting thing happened. Beautiful gardens of his Jacksonville clients caught his attention and little by little the oyster business changed to horticulture.

In the garden of one of his Jacksonville customers, Gerbing discovered the beauty of camellias. Instantly he knew he wanted to grow them. Always a shrewd businessman, his oysters became the currency for his camellia obsession, as he arranged for subsequent deliveries to that customer to be paid for in camellia plants.

In 1923, Gus Gerbing began two new chapters in his life. He opened the Gerbing Camellia Nursery in Fernandina, and he married Azilda Elaine Fyfe, a strikingly beautiful young woman. Born in New York City in 1903, she had moved with her family to the north Florida city when she was 16 and was working in an oyster cannery in Jacksonville when she and Gus met. The couple found the distance between Fernandina and Jacksonville close enough for courtship, and were soon married.

Gerbing's oyster business continued and spawned Gerbing's Oyster Restaurant where Azilda helped him by waiting tables. Her tips were mostly in silver dollars, and she saved them all, eventually dividing them among their five children when they were grown. Elaine was born a year after Gus and Azilda were married, and George followed a year later. With their arrivals, Azilda's career changed from caring for customers to caring for her home and family. Two more daughters, Dorothy and Lucille, and finally another son, David, were born. The Gerbings tragically lost David when he was killed his senior year in high school while attending a training class for electricians. It was an especially difficult time for Azilda, a quiet, restrained woman.

Meanwhile, Gus had left the oyster business, closed the restaurant, and, in 1932, turned to his nursery full time. He specialized in camellias, but also established a spectacular 20-acre show garden, Gerbings Gardens, in Fernandina Beach. Its 60-cent admission allowed the visitor to enjoy an 800-footlong windbreak of 'Sara Frost' camellias, a 4-acre sunken garden planted with bulbs, and an amphitheater composed of 25,000 azaleas, intermingled with other southern staples such as live oaks and magnolias. For those who were less enchanted by the gardens, Gerbing offered all-day fishing on his nearby 800' ocean pier for 50 cents. Before it closed in 1950, Gerbings Gardens was one of the most popular tourist attractions in northeast Florida.

Among the many azaleas blooming each spring in Gerbings Gardens was the lovely Southern Indica azalea 'George L. Taber.' In the spring of 1936, Gus discovered a white-flowered sport on the Taber azalea. and propagated it from cuttings. After several years of testing, he introduced it as 'Mrs. G. G. Gerbing' in honor of his wife, his constant and steadfast "silent partner." Azilda's namesake azalea is one of the most cold tolerant of the Southern Indica types and typically grows 8' to 10' tall and equally wide. The large white flowers have made it one of the most popular plants in southern gardens.

Gus Gerbing's camellia passion led him to become a charter and active member of the American Camellia Society. In 1943, he wrote about his extensive experiences growing camellias in the book *Camellias by G.G. Gerbing*, the first comprehensive, all-color camellia book in America. Literary organizations such as the International Mark Twain Society and the Eugene Field Society of American Authors recognized the work with tributes, which caused Gerbing to remark, "Not bad for a country boy who didn't quite make the sixth grade." He dedicated his book to Azilda.

Gerbing sold his nursery in 1946, four years before he closed Gerbings Gardens. The Gerbing Nursery, however, remained a viable business until the land was sold for the development of Amelia Island Plantation in 1973. Gus moved on to new pursuits but continued to grow plants, especially annuals, for local outlets. His expertise in horticulture was sought from around the world, and he continued to share his passion for his favorite plants until he died from cancer in 1982. Azilda lived to be 92, and until she died in 1995, she found her greatest joy in being with her family, especially her grandchildren and great-grandchildren.

Until he retired, Gerbing's eldest son, George, worked with camellias and also developed a widespread excellent reputation. When George decided he would no longer sell camellias, the Gerbing family was officially out of the plant business. Although camellias were the Gerbing's signature plants, the well-known Southern Indica azalea, 'Mrs. G. G. Gerbing' became the flag-bearer of the Gerbing Nursery, a Fernandina institution that played a significant role in American horticultural history.

References

Barnes, Asa, and Sevell, John N. "In Appreciation of G. G. Gerbing," *American Camellia Society Yearbook*. 1981: xiii-xvi.

Gerbing, G.G. *Camellias by G. G. Gerbing*. Fernandina: G. G. Gerbing:1950.

"Gerbing's Gardens, Fernandina Beach, Florida." 1948. Post card folder.

Abelia x *grandiflora*
'John Creech'

Aquilegia canadensis
'Corbett'

Asarum shuttleworthii
'Callaway'

Aster
'Hella Lacy'

Calycanthus floridus
'Athens'

Photo by Vincent Simeone

Photo by Allen Bush

Calycanthus floridus
'Michael Lindsey'

Camellia japonica
'Betty Sheffield'

Photo by Clyde Copeland

Photo by Clyde Copeland

Camellia japonica
'Betty Sheffield
Supreme'

Citrus x *limonia*
'Meyer'
(*Citrus* x *meyeri*)

Clematis viticella
'Betty Corning'

Clethra alnifolia
'Hummingbird'

Daphne x *burkwoodii*
'Carol Mackie'

*Dianthus
gratianopolitanus*
'Bath's Pink'

Photo by Allan Armitage

Photo by Allan Armitage

Dianthus plumarius
'ItSaul White'

Echinacea purpurea
'Kim's Knee-High'

Photo by Allan Armitage

Photo by Marc Laviana

Echinacea purpurea
'Kim's Mop Head'

Erica x *watsonii*
'Dorothy Metheny'

Fothergilla gardenii
'Jane Platt'

Fothergilla major
'Mount Airy'

Hamamelis x *intermedia*
'Arnold Promise'

Heuchera
'Eco Magnififolia'

Heuchera
'Molly Bush'

Heuchera
'Montrose Ruby'

Hosta sieboldiana
'Frances Williams'

Hosta
'Solar Flare'

Hydrangea arborescens
'Annabelle'

Hydrangea macrophylla
'Dooley'

Hydrangea macrophylla
'Wave Hill'

Ilex x
'Doctor Kassab'

Ilex x
'Emily Bruner'

Ilex x
'Nellie R. Stevens'
(original plant)

Itea virginica
'Henry's Garnet'

Lantana camara
'Miss Huff'

Leptospermum scoparium
'Helene Strybing'

Leucanthemum x *superbum*
'Ryan's Daisy'
('Becky')

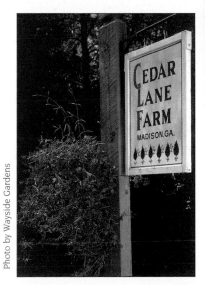

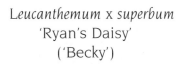

Lonicera sempervirens
'Cedar Lane'

Lonicera sempervirens
'Sulphurea'

Photo by Jane Symmes

Photo by Allan Armitage

Lysimachia congestiflora
'Eco Dark Satin'

Magnolia grandiflora
'Bracken's Brown Beauty'

Photo by Vincent Simeone

Photo by Claudia Covington

Magnolia grandiflora
'Claudia Wannamaker'
(original plant)

Magnolia macrophylla
'Julian Hill'

Magnolia stellata
'Rosea Jane Platt'

Monarda
'Gardenview Scarlet'

Oenothera glazioviana
'Tina James'

Phlox x
'Chattahoochee'

Photo by Allan Armitage

Photo by Allan Armitage

Phlox divaricata
'Fuller's White'

Phlox paniculata
'David'

Photo by Allan Armitage

Photo by Iseli Nursery, Inc.

Picea pungens
'Fat Albert'

Picea pungens
'Iseli Fastigiate'

Picea pungens
'Iseli Foxtail'

Pulmonaria
'Benediction'

Pulmonaria
'Roy Davidson'

Rhododendron
'Alexander'

Rhododendron
'Galle's Choice'

Rhododendron
'George L. Taber'

Rhododendron
'Mrs. G. G. Gerbing'

Rosa
'Blush Noisette'

Rosa
'Burbank'

Rosa
'Champneys'
Pink Cluster'

Ruellia britonniana
'Katie'

Sedum
'John Creech'

Trachelospermum
jasminoides
'Madison'

Veronica
'Goodness Grows'

Veronica
'Sunny Border Blue'

Acknowledgments
George Gerbing
Louise Gerbing
Stacy Catron-Sullivan
Anne Walton

Photograph courtesy of Louise Gerbing.

GOODNESS GROWS

Marc Richardson and Rick Berry

Veronica 'Goodness Grows'

M arc Richardson and Rick Berry began Goodness Grows
Nursery in Crawford, Georgia, in 1979, and grew their small
plot into a highly successful business noted for its perennials.
In fact, much of the credit for the upsurge of interest in perennials for the Southeast must be given to them.

Richardson and Berry realized that many garden-worthy
plants could be grown in southeastern gardens, especially
southeastern natives, and that many were perennials in that
region. By pouring over the writings of Elizabeth Lawrence and
William Hunt, as well as canvassing family and friends, they discovered many exceptional plants. Marc's grandmother was a
veteran gardener in Donaldsonville, Georgia, and introduced
him to many of the plants she loved, such as the white ginger
lily, Hedychium coronarium. When the two men discovered that
most of these plants were totally unavailable in garden centers,
they purchased seeds or collected them from roadside plants,
and procured plants from friends and neighbors. With their new
discoveries, they created their own magnificent garden and
began growing a supply for Rick's landscape business. Soon

gardeners from all over the South were hearing about their fine plants and traveling to Crawford to make their purchases.

The two young men had not planned to become nurserymen when they met at the University of Georgia in Athens. Marc studied biology and Rick majored in math education. After graduation Marc became an assistant greenhouse manager at the university and Rick became a landscaper. Their nursery business evolved from their first outlet at a weekend flea market in Atlanta where they sold their plants from Crawford. Soon they developed a significant following with customers frequently making comments like, "My grandmother used to grow that," or, "What is that wonderful plant?" At the same time, in the early 1980s, the Atlanta Botanical Garden began its semiannual plant sale. Organizers knew of Rick and Marc's flea market business and asked them to supply a truckload of plants for the sale. One truckload turned into three. At the end of the sale they enjoyed an even greater reputation in the gardening community.

Richardson and Berry also point out important developments taking place in the Horticulture Department of the University of Georgia. Allan Armitage and Michael Dirr had just arrived, and these professors not only supported the efforts at Goodness Grows, but were also dispersing greater plant knowledge to southern gardeners. The demand for Southeastern plants grew to the point that Marc and Rick both left their former jobs to concentrate on building a much needed Southeastern nursery and garden center.

Marc's experience at the greenhouses at Georgia, especially his work with germinating seeds for wildflower trials, gave him knowledge of propagating and plant selection, which he continues to use at the nursery today. Rick is the "up front" man and works with the consumers and dispenses advice and information. Customers leave the nursery delighted with their fine plants and satisfied that they have the information they need to succeed.

Veronica 'Goodness Grows' is the standard-bearer of Richardson and Berry's business. The original plant was a chance seedling found growing in an area near a plot containing *Veronica alpina* 'Alba' and *Veronica spicata* 'Rosea.' The resulting offspring had the low-growing habit (10"–12") of the former and the long blue racemes of the latter. With its persistent flowering habit, *Veronica* 'Goodness Grows' has become a popular garden addition since its introduction in 1982.

Richardson and Berry were also instrumental in introducing *Dianthus* 'Bath's Pink' from Jane Bath and *Lysimachia congestiflora* 'Eco Dark Satin' from Don Jacobs's Eco-Gardens in Decatur, Georgia. Rick tells the story that he and Marc were on a garden tour in Atlanta when they first admired the lysimachia. Coincidentally, Jacobs was also there and suggested that Goodness Grows put his plant into production. They did, and this plant, as well as 'Bath's Pink,' have been widely successful.

Another of the nursery's special plants is a yarrow (*Achillea millefolium*) called 'Oertel's Rose,' a beautiful repeat-blooming dwarf plant with pink-and-white flowers. Mae Oertel, a stroke patient confined to a wheel chair, presented this flower to Marc and Rick to express her appreciation for the great pleasure she derived from her regular visits to Goodness Grows. Although Mae brought the plant from Missouri, it has become an excellent addition to the southeastern garden palette.

As the gardening community has demanded new plants, some duplication in introductions is inevitable. Goodness Grows introduced an excellent strong-stemmed shasta daisy (*Leucanthemum* x *superbum*) that had been shared with them by their friend, Ryan Gainey, a well-known Atlanta gardener, designer, and author. The original plant was given to Gainey by Mrs. Mary Ann Gatlin of Decatur, Georgia, who reported that it had been growing in her mother's garden since the 1930s. After evaluation the plant, Goodness Grows sold it as 'Ryan's Daisy' and listed it in their 1989 catalogue. At about the same time, nurseryman Bill Funkhouser discovered the plant in the garden of Becky and Jimmy Stewart, garden designers in Decatur. Unaware of the Goodness Grows introduction, he sold the plant in his retail nursery as 'Becky'. The plant was introduced as

'Becky' to the Perennial Plant Symposium in Atlanta in 1990 and in the early 1990s appeared as 'Becky' in the Wayside Gardens catalogue. Goodness Grows continues to list it as they first received it, as 'Ryan's Daisy'. There is no doubt the two plants are the same, but regardless of the name, this plant is far superior to other tall white-flowered shasta daisies on the market.

Lantana 'Miss Huff' is another Goodness Grows introduction. It is a thornless shrubby lantana that from early summer until frost is covered with blended yellow, orange, and pink flower clusters. Most lantanas are tender in north Georgia, but the nurserymen noticed this particular lantana returning every year in their neighbor's garden. Their neighbor was "Miss Ruby" Huff, the wife of a local farmer in Crawford, and her lantana grew amidst tomatoes and snowball bushes. She did not know the origin of the shrub, but she provided them with a cutting. Naturally, when Richardson and Berry decided to put this plant into the trade, they named it for their neighbor.

The nursery outgrew its space in Crawford and, in 1985 Marc and Rick moved the nursery a few miles down the road to its present location in Lexington, Georgia. Goodness Grows continues to provide plants that have tested tried and true for Southeastern garden conditions, and, in addition offers many that may be found thriving in gardens everywhere. The nursery's outstanding catalogue lists their extensive offerings, including *Veronica* 'Goodness Grows,' the plant which symbolizes their immense contribution to gardening.

Acknowledgments
Rick Berry
Marc Richardson

Photograph by Linda Copeland.

KIM HAWKS

Kim Hawks

Echinacea purpurea 'Kim's Knee-High'

Knee-high" is a relative anatomical measurement, which immediately conjures up someone, or something, short in nature. In this case the knee belongs to an energetic woman named Kim Hawks, who stands about 5'1" tall, and her short, compact namesake plant is perfectly named. The purple cone-flower in question is up to a foot shorter than other selections of the plant and also provides long blooming bright pink flowers and handsome green foliage. The story begins with Kim's visit to the garden of her friends, Becky and Jimmy Stewart.

When the Stewarts showed her an unusually short cone-flower in their Decatur, Georgia garden, she asked them for some seeds to take back to Niche Gardens, her nursery in North Carolina. Over several years she grew populations of the plant and from each group of seedlings Kim selected the shortest and most compact specimens. Believing her final selection was a plant with promise, she sent it to her friend Pierre Bennerup at Sunny Border Nurseries in Connecticut. When the plant tested equally favorably for him, they decided it should be a Niche Gardens/Sunny Border introduction for 1999.

It was Bill Cullina, the nursery manager at Niche Gardens at that time, who suggested the whimsical name. 'Kim's Knee-High' was instantly successful with gardeners and landscapers here and abroad. In 2000, it was selected as the Best New Perennial of the Year in the Netherlands.

Raised in Raleigh, North Carolina, Kim Hawks's background foreshadowed her career in horticulture. Her father, a forester who developed the urban tree program for Raleigh, taught Kim a love of trees and nature, and her mother and grandmother introduced her to the the joys of gardening. Not surprisingly, she attended North Carolina State University and majored in horticulture, and realized her passion for plant propagation. After she graduated in 1977, she worked for several businesses, including landscaping companies, retail garden centers, and greenhouse growers, all experiences that would help with her major career move.

Kim's delight in plant propagation and fondness for the native plants of the area, led her to dream of owning a nursery. She found seven acres of wooded land near Chapel Hill, North Carolina, and opened her nursery business in 1986. Above the door she placed a sign reading, "Niche Gardens", an appellation describing her singular focus on growing unique garden plants. Interestingly, the name came to her one evening while standing over the sink washing dishes. Staring out the window and musing about her plan, she promised herself she would grow beautiful plants for garden niches, and then realized her distinctive mission would also make a terrific name.

Niche Gardens quickly became an outstanding and highly successful specialty nursery, one admired throughout the horticulture industry and gardening circles. With an emphasis on North American natives, Kim designed and maintains several creative display gardens on the property. In addition to providing the seeds for Kim's next crop of specialty plants, these areas also serve as trial areas and space to experiment with interesting plant combinations.

'Kim's Knee-High' went on to produce other coneflowers,

one of which was also introduced by Niche Gardens and Sunny Border Nurseries. Seeds from the original plant yielded a pure white, compact form with slightly ragged petals, and was released in spring 2001. In affectionate homage to Kim's hair style, Pierre Bennerup named the plant 'Kim's Mop Head'.

'Kim's Knee-High' and 'Kim's Mop Head' are fine tributes to a terrific lady who created a wonderful nursery.

References

Tate, Martha. "Think Summer with a Coneflower That's Compact." *Home & Garden* /The Atlanta Journal-Constitution. January 1, 2001: 6.
http://www.nichegdn.com

Acknowledgments

Kim Hawks
Luc Klinkhamer
Marc Laviana

Photograph by Virginia R. Weiler.

MARY GIBSON HENRY

Mary Gibson Henry

Itea virginica 'Henry's Garnet'

At five feet one inch tall, Mary Gibson Henry was diminutive in stature, but her accomplishments as a field botanist and plantswoman were on the grandest scale. The Henry Foundation for Botanical Research in Gladwyne, Pennsylvania, is the living legacy of her life's work.

Mary Henry's ancestry and love for plants is traceable to the founding fathers of Philadelphia. Her great-grandfather, George Pepper, was a member of the first Council of the Pennsylvania Horticulture Society, and her grandfather Gibson was an enthusiastic greenhouse gardener. Mary was born in Jenkinstown, Pennsylvania, on August 15, 1884, and grew up in Philadelphia. Her parents, Susan Worrel Pepper and John Howard Gibson, had no garden at their home in the city, but during summer outings introduced their three children to more pastoral settings.

Mary's real love for the outdoors came from her father's teachings and stories about camping and hunting. Learning to fire a gun was one of the lessons which later became an invaluable skill on her wilderness expeditions. Sadly, her father died when she was only 11, but throughout her life Mary displayed his appreciation for exploration and the wonders of nature.

Mary graduated from the Agnes Irwin School in Philadelphia in 1902. Although she did not continue college she combined an insatiable curiosity with the values of discipline and hard work learned from her family. This strength of character and the Gibson family's social status allowed her to enjoy a privileged and productive life full of adventure and travel.

After high school she journeyed west with her aunt, Mary Klett Gibson, for her first glimpse of the Rocky Mountains and the Grand Canyon. When she was 23, her mother took the family to France, where Mary climbed to the summit of Mont Blanc, an unusual exploit for a woman at that time, in the years before women even had the right to vote.

In 1909, Mary Gibson married a fellow outdoorsman, John Norman Henry, a Philadelphia physician. Fittingly, the couple spent their wedding trip camping and canoeing. For 17 years the Henrys lived in urban Philadelphia until they purchased 95 acres and built a home in Gladwyne, a town in the countryside west of the city. In 1926, with their family of five children, they moved into a beautiful stone house with a nearby greenhouse for Mary, who then began her horticultural career in earnest.

Only one year later, tragedy struck when the Henrys' six-year-old son, Frederick, died. At this difficult time, Mary sought refuge and comfort in her gardening. Through two important books she had read, *The Travels of William Bartram* and J. K. Small's *Flora of the Southeastern United States*, Mary had become interested in American native plants. Wishing to grow them in her Gladwyne garden, she soon discovered that these plants were unavailable for purchase. Her solution? She would visit native habitats to find them herself.

Her husband supported her in every conceivable way. Norman Henry arranged for a specially outfitted car consisting of a rooftop "attic" where equipment could be carried, an insulated and ventilated rear compartment for newly collected plants, and a bookcase and electrically lit desk inside. The family's handyman, gardener, and chauffeur, Ernest Perks usually drove the vehicle for Mary's expeditions, traveling ahead so that he could meet her when she arrived by train. They journeyed up and down the Atlantic Coastal Plain, over the Piedmont Plateau, and, later, along the eastern and western slopes of the Appalachian Mountains. Incredibly, Mary Henry would travel the North American continent studying and collecting native flora for more than 40 years.

Mary Gibson Henry was serious about plant collecting. She assembled thousands of herbarium specimens, which were given to the Academy of Natural Sciences in Philadelphia, and kept careful records and diaries. As early as the middle of the twentieth century, one diary entry reveals her advocacy for conservation: "Certain localities show the dire need for a greater conservation than is now practiced." She further commented, "I soon learned that rare and beautiful plants can only be found in places that are difficult of access." Mary endured the elements and risked danger from threatening wildlife and, occasionally, threatening people. Regardless, she considered every minute an interesting and exciting adventure.

By taking her newfound American treasures back to her garden at Gladwyne, Henry achieved her original goal. The natives were planted in a naturalistic setting among plants from other explorers and other continents on the property's sloping hillsides that became Mary's "Wild Garden." From an outcrop of rugged rocks crowning the highest point, she also created her "Rock Garden." People came from all over to visit and see plants they could find in no other garden.

In November 1954, on a trip to Coweta County, Georgia, Mary collected an outstanding form of Virginia sweetspire, *Itea virginica*. The plant's deep red autumn foliage color caught her eye and she described it on her herbarium sample, "leaves bright, glossy, carmine." She took the plant back to Gladwyne and planted it beside the driveway that passed through the property. Over the years the Henry Foundation distributed the plant to various nurseries and horticultural institutions, and thereby it made its way to the Scott Arboretum at Swarthmore College in Media, Pennsylvania. It grew there essentially unnoticed until horticulturist Michael Dirr spotted it in its autumn finery in the fall of 1982. He suggested to Judy Zuk, the Coordinator of Education of the Scott Arboretum at the time, that the plant be named and introduced.

Consultation with the Henry Foundation yielded the name 'Henry's Garnet,' attributing the plant's discovery to Mary Gibson Henry and celebrating its fine garnet autumn color. Because garnet is the school color of Swarthmore, the name is also associated with the arboretum there. Woodlanders Nursery in Aiken, South Carolina, first sold it as 'Selected Form,' but offered it as 'Henry's Garnet' in its 1986–87 catalogue.

Virginia sweetspire is native to floodplains from New Jersey to Florida. Adaptable to sun or light shade and dry or wet conditions, these shrubs bear long arching branches and fragrant white flowers up to six inches in length. According to Dirr, Henry's selection is "superior to the species" for both its fall color and its flowers. In 1988, 'Henry's Garnet' was presented the prestigious Styer Award (now the Gold Medal) from the Pennsylvania Horticultural Society, undeniable proof of Mary Henry's eye for selecting outstanding plants.

Another of Henry's popular plants grown in gardens today is *Phlox* x 'Chattahoochee.' The Chattahoochee River flows from the mountains of north Georgia southward along the Alabama-Georgia border until it crosses the state of Florida and empties into the Gulf of Mexico. Henry visited this river valley in Florida at its southernmost reaches near the town of Chattahoochee. There she found the handsome phlox specimen that she believed had migrated southward from the river's source. She theorized that the migratory plants would grow well in more northerly areas, and was rewarded with successful populations in her Gladwyne garden. The Henry discovery, which was determined to be a cross between *Phlox divaricata* var. *laphamii* and the pale purple–flowered downy *Phlox pilosa*, has lavender flowers with a striking purple eye and leaves that are longer, wider, and darker green when compared with the parents. Although it is not an especially vigorous plant, *Phlox* x 'Chattahoochee' is outstanding and beautiful when in flower.

On several occasions Mary was joined on her botanical adventures by members of her family. In 1931, she and Norman took their four children to explore an unmapped region of British Columbia in western Canada, simply known then as the "Tropical Valley," a name referring to the location of numerous hot springs. With camping provisions, 58 horses, and an additional nine men, the Henrys spent "80 thrilling days" in this unknown northern wilderness. Mary's diaries describe dramatic climate swings and difficult terrain, but her delight in the natural beauty was the central theme of her recordings. In Mary Henry's words, this place was "where the sky is the only ceiling and the ground is strewn with sparkling flowers." K. F. McCusker, a topographer provided by the Topographical Survey of Canada, accompanied this most unusual family expedition. While mapping the uncharted territory he discovered a new peak and called it Mt. Mary Henry, an honor formalized by the Department of Lands of British Columbia in 1931.

With her daughter, Josephine, Mary Henry made three more trips to this magnificent place, all the while collecting propagules, seeds, and dried specimens, including several thousand herbarium specimens for the Royal Botanic Garden of Edinburgh and the Academy of Natural Sciences in Philadelphia. In 1948 she received the Mungo Park Medal from the Royal Scottish Geographical Society for "Explorations in Northern British Columbia."

Mary Henry's work has been honored many times. She received the Pennsylvania Horticultural Society's Schaeffer Gold Medal in 1941 for "notable contributions to horticulture" and the Silver Medal from the Massachusetts Horticultural Society in 1946 for an exhibit of *Lilium philadelphicum*. As a plant breeder,

Henry was interested in the *Hymenocallis* species native to the United States and in the breeding of x *Crytanthus*. For her work with these, she was presented with the William Herbert Medal in 1950 for "her outstanding achievements toward the advancement of the *Amaryllids*." In 1956, the University of Pennsylvania, her late husband's alma mater, presented her with an extraordinary recognition for an amateur: the honorary degree of Master of Science, citing her contributions to science and "to man's knowledge in botany, horticulture, and geography." Henry was also an honorary fellow of the Botanical Society of Edinburgh and closely affiliated with many other botanical organizations.

As Mary Henry's reputation grew, her home and research facilities in Gladwyne became a favorite gathering place for botanists from around the globe. She presented many lectures in North America and abroad and even found time to write numerous articles about her research and plant discoveries. In 1948, to perpetuate her garden and her work, Mary Henry and her children established the Henry Foundation for Botanical Research on 16 acres of their land. Its mission was to collect and preserve choice, rare, and endangered New World plants and to make them available to botanic gardens and responsible growers. When Mary Henry died in 1967, her daughter, Josephine deNanerede Henry, became the Director. Since 1996, two of her granddaughters have continued to implement the foundation's mission: Susan Pepper Treadway as Director, and Betsey Warren Davis as Curator of the Mary Gibson Henry Collection Records.

"Mamo," as Henry was known to her 12 grandchildren, spent her lifetime creating a legacy of knowledge about North American plants. She was a superb plant explorer and a significant contributor to botanical and horticultural knowledge. The plants she discovered, including 'Henry's Garnet' sweetspire and 'Chattahoochee' phlox are beautiful reminders of this amazing twentieth-century woman.

References

Dirr, Michael A. *Manual of Woody Landscape Plants.* 5th edition. Champaign: Stipes, 1998.

Henry, Mary Gibson. "Mary Gibson Henry, an Autobiography." *Plant Life.* Jan., Apr., Jul., & Oct., 1950: 11-30.

Acknowledgments

Andrew Bunting
Betsey W. Davis
Michael Dirr
Beth Gainer
Josephine deN. Henry
Robert B. McCartney
Susan Pepper Treadway
Judy Zuk

Photograph courtesy of the Henry Foundation for Botanical Research.

POLLY HILL

Polly Hill

Magnolia macrophylla 'Julian Hill'

Polly Hill became one of the most highly accomplished gardeners in the United States. At the age of 50, when most peoples are slowing down, she began to develop the garden that has since become the Polly Hill Arboretum on Martha's Vineyard, an island off the coast of Massachusetts. In 1957, when her mother died, Polly became the steward of her family's summer home, Barnard's Inn Farm, originally purchased by her parents, Margaret Keen and Howard Butcher in 1926. Realizing the opportunity the 47-acre property afforded, she decided to turn the old sheep farm into a garden where she could grow plants previously unknown on the island.

Polly and her husband, Julian Hill, an organic chemist for the DuPont Company, lived with their family during the school year in Wilmington, Delaware, an area rich in horticultural traditions and opportunities. As Polly's enthusiasm for plants and gardening developed, she enrolled in horticulture and botany courses at nearby Longwood Gardens and the University of Delaware, where she gained the knowledge she needed to lay the foundation for her exciting new venture.

Polly believed a theory that plants grown from seed in a specific location outdoors might adapt better to that location than those transplanted from elsewhere and extend the plant's limits of hardiness. She set about collecting seeds from sources of all kinds, raising them in outdoor nursery beds at Barnard's Inn Farm, and looking for the most promising plants among the seedlings. Eventually those seedlings successfully produced trees and shrubs formerly thought unsuitable for the climate on Martha's Vineyard. Many of the mature plants now residing in the arboretum were started in that manner. From this work, Polly Hill introduced more than 75 plants to ornamental horticulture.

There is no question Polly enjoys naming plants for people she cherishes and many of her introductions were named in this manner. This custom provides numerous reminders of her family and friends as she wanders along the arboretum paths. And, because she has graciously shared her plants with the horticulture trade, Polly's named plants have become widely recognized and enjoyed in gardens around the globe.

Azaleas make up a large part of Hill's introductions. She refers to them as North Tisbury Hybrids, so named because of her property's location in the town of North Tisbury on Martha's Vineyard. However, most of them originated because of her visits to Japan. After graduating from Vassar College with a degree in liberal arts in 1928, she taught the next year at Tokyo Joshi Daigaku, the Tokyo Women's College. While there, she made note of ground-covering azaleas unlike any she knew at home. When Polly returned to Japan for a visit in 1956, Russell Seibert, the director of Longwood Gardens, arranged for her to meet Tsuneshige Rokujo of Tokyo, a physician and collector and breeder of rhododendrons. Their meeting led to a lifelong friendship through correspondence and resulted in Polly's acquiring and introducing many new ground-covering azaleas to America.

In 1957, Rokujo sent her a gift of five rooted cuttings of "new Gumpo seedlings" from dwarf, rare plants which had been cultivated in Japan for more than 100 years. Polly named these

99

plants for five Japanese friends: 'Eiko San,' Polly's mentor, guide, and fellow teacher when she taught in Tokyo; 'Matsuyo' a student of Polly's in Tokyo who later worked for the Japanese government in home economics; 'Midori' Nishikawa, another student who became a long time friend; 'Yaye' Hirooka, a friend from Polly's year in Tokyo; and 'Yuka,' also a former pupil who later taught English while serving the YWCA in Tokyo. These plants were the beginning of the North Tisbury collection.

Rokujo continued to make crosses of dwarf azaleas in Japan and sent Polly many of the resulting seeds. She selected the best performers from the resultant seedlings, naming many for family members. 'Jeff Hill,' with light red flowers; 'Joseph Hill,' with bright red blooms; and 'Louisa,' with pink blossoms, are named for her three children, but other family members were also included. 'Gabrielle Hill' (her daughter-in-law) has a delicately ruffled violet flower, and 'Bartlett' (her daughter-in-law's family) has a bloom of medium salmon pink. A plant with a lightly ruffled, bright rose flower became 'Michael Hill' (grandson), and a 2 1/4"-wide, red-flowered dwarf hybrid was named for her red-haired grandson, Alexander Hill. Also adorned with red hair, granddaughter Susannah's name was given to a specimen that, when in flower, is covered by small double red blooms which look like tiny roses. All of these North Tisbury Azaleas have been registered with the American Rhododendron Society and introduced into American horticulture.

Hill named two other plants for her grandchildren. For Corinna Borden, she selected the palest pink-flowered azalea *Rhododendron kaempferi* var. *leucanthum* from Rokujo seedlings. According to Polly, the soft color of this plant "calms strident combinations of clashing colors" even better than white, a lovely attribute she associates with her granddaughter. Polly selected *Rhododendron makinoi* 'Lydia Richards.' from seedlings distributed by the Rhododendron Society Seed Exchange. Polly notes 'Lydia Richards, is a striking plant with new leaves blanketed by heavy off-white indumentum (hairs) followed by "huge trusses of rich pink flowers."

Members of Hill's family have found their names also given to non-Rhododendron species. Lydia, her youngest grandchild, told her grandmother she wished to have a "a big tree" named for her. In 1968, Rokujo sent Polly three bare-rooted saplings of *Magnolia hypoleuca*, and Polly named one for Lydia. The tree is upright, almost fastigiate and bears fragrant creamy white flowers with pink outer tepals. Lydia still enjoys her namesake in front of her home in Washington, D.C.

In 1960, Polly was given a large pod of bright red seeds of *Magnolia macrophylla*. She selected one of the seedlings to plant in a protected area of her garden. The resulting tree flowered in only nine years and became the one she named 'Julian Hill.' Her husband preferred large white blossoms, and she felt this plant with its 9"–11", fragrant white flowers was the ideal plant to bear his name. Thriving beyond its northernmost limits for hardiness, 'Julian Hill' has become a popular tree at the Polly Hill Arboretum and a handsome memorial to Julian, Polly's husband, a chemist of note, who was one of the first developers of nylon. Julian died in 1996. Their 64 years of marriage was a "merry time" according to Polly.

Of all of the plants Polly has named for friends, one of her greatest challenges was to find a plant to honor Tsuneshige Rokujo, her friend and colleague for 42 years. In 1972, when Henry Skinner, director of the United States Arboretum gave Polly a rooted cutting of a fragrant, medium pink-flowered American rhododendron hybrid, a cross he had made of *R. serrulatum* x *R. prunifolium*, Polly felt she had found the plant worthy to bear Rokujo's name. When she told her friend about the plant, he requested Polly give it his entire name. Polly realized Americans would have difficulty with the pronunciaition, so she asked the American Rhododendron Society to accept both his name and his nickname "Shigi." Her request was granted, and, in 1986, both names were registered. Polly's hope is that this late-blooming fragrant azalea will become popular, and her special friend, who died in 1998 at the age of 78, will be remembered in American gardens by her lovely selection, *Rhododendron* 'Tsuneshige Rokujo' (syn. 'Shigi').

Polly's plant introductions and her experimentation have received much acclaim. In 1990 she received the Arthur Hoyt Scott Medal and Award, and in 1997 she was awarded the Garden Club of America Medal of Honor. Her meticulous record-keeping of her plant accessions and gardening activities led to her selection for the Plant Records Committee of the American Horticultural Society. Hill's arboretum became one of the first private gardens to have computerized records.

However, the finest tribute to her work was the creation of the Polly Hill Arboretum, the result of an effort spearheaded by David H. Smith, philanthropist, conservationist, and resident of Martha's Vineyard. Now all of Polly's gardens at Barnard's Inn Farm are protected from future development by of the Commonwealth of Massachusetts. The 60-acre arboretum has been incorporated as a nonprofit organization committed to preserving Hill's legacy, a fact that caused Polly to declare, "I just think I'm the luckiest creature who ever lived. Now, my plants will be cared for and the public will feel welcomed... enjoying it with me and sharing it with me." Additionally, all gardeners may share in her outstanding legacy by growing the plants she has selected and introduced from this magnificent landscape on Martha's Vineyard.

References

Driskoll, Kathi Scrizzi. "Preserving Polly's Dream," *Cape Cod Times* June 11, 1999: Outdoors.

Hill, Polly "My Plant Introductions." The Polly Hill Arboretum, May 2000.

Hill, Polly. "Polly Hill and Her Arboretum," Video Tape. The Polly Hill Arboretum.

Ockenga, Starr. *Earth on her Hands: The American Woman in her Garden*. New York: Clarkson Potter, Inc.. 1998.

Acknowledgment
Polly Hill

Photograph by Linda Copeland.

ANDRÉ ISELI

André Iseli

Picea pungens 'Iseli Foxtail'

André Iseli is a philosopher, artist, dreamer and a terrific plantsman. With this special combination of talents, he became the owner and president of Iseli Nursery in Boring, Oregon. However, the road that led him into the nursery business is full of many twists and turns.

Born in Switzerland in the town of La Chaux-de-Fonds on the French border, André was eight years old when his parents immigrated to the United States and settled in Portland, Oregon. André and his brother, Jean, grew up in the nursery business started by their parents whose work and teachings made a lasting impression on their sons. Recalling with affection the red geraniums and blue lobelias spilling from his mother's window boxes in Switzerland, André credits her with his love for plants. He describes his dad as having "a willing heart, a beautiful work ethic, and a thirst for knowledge", which became the core of André's lifelong philosophy. He believes that what life gives depends on what is given, and that "nothing is impossible to a willing heart!"

André Iseli remained in Oregon and received a bachelor's degree from Linfield College, a small liberal arts school in

McMinnville. However, for his masters degree he returned to Europe and attended the Sorbonne in Paris, where he studied theater arts and painting. He became a passionate artist in the surrealist style, perhaps a forecast of his future work with plants.

At the beginning of the Korean War Iseli was in France, and there, he learned he had been drafted by the Army. He reported to Fort Lewis in Washington for duty. Just before being sent to Korea, André learned the Army was looking for people with radio skills. Excited by the possibility for using his previous training, he immediately volunteered and was sent to Japan for a year and a half tour of duty. André "fell in love with the Japanese people and their culture" and developed a particular interest in the indigenous art of Japanese Bonsai, later evidenced in his work at Iseli Nursery. After returning to the United States, he continued to work in the radio industry, then moved into television and motion pictures.

After four years of working as an actor Iseli decided to become a producer. He needed additional funds to make this change, and, without losing a step, became a successful investment banker in California. Among his many clients was a corporation considering the sale of a 40-acre rhododendron nursery in Oregon. Iseli advised the client he would help find a buyer for the nursery and went to see it himself. By then, his infatuation with Hollywood had diminished and he found himself intrigued with the thought of owning the nursery. In 1974, only three months after his first visit, he bought what became Iseli Nursery.

André enlisted his younger brother to run the nursery. Jean enthusiastically took on the job, and, within a few months, had earned the respect of the nursery industry. André, in the meantime, built an office for his investment banking business on the nursery site. When he moved to Oregon from California, the future of the nursery was forged.

Dwarf conifers were the Iselis' passion, and together they pledged to build the finest nursery of its kind in the world. To accomplish their goal, Jean ran the daily operations, and André made long-range plans and took care of legal, financial, and advertising responsibilities. The nursery prospered and developed an outstanding reputation. The brothers continued to run the nursery together until Jean's untimely death from a heart attack in 1987.

Following this terrible tragedy, André was forced to find a replacement for Jean as the nursery's leader. Finding no one suitable, he decided on yet another career change, and became the president of Iseli Nursery himself.

The company's slogan, "Where the beauty of nature meets the artistry of man," illustrates André's vision for the nursery. He also believes that "a thing of beauty is a joy forever." Plants from Iseli Nursery reflect these thoughts and enhance its reputation for high standards of quality within the horticulture industry. Iseli was one of the first major nurseries to include Bonsai as part of its inventory and, in addition, offers many plants that are shaped and combined into artistic forms and topiaries. The nursery catalogue, itself a thing of beauty, contains listings for a large number of signature plants. Their discovery and subsequent naming provide intriguing stories.

In the early days, Iseli Nursery purchased large numbers of Colorado blue spruce, *Picea pungens*. From subsequent seedling populations, Iseli made three distinctive selections; *Picea pungens* 'Fat Albert' is one of these. This blue spruce was found in 1976, and according to the nursery's catalogue, it is the "fattest, bluest, most perfect BIG blue spruce grown". It has a dependable pyramidal shape and blue color. The name was borrowed from a Bill Cosby television show character often introduced by the line "hey, hey, hey...here comes fat Albert." André says that his brother was opposed to plant patents, whereby the nursery would receive royalties for every 'Fat Albert' produced, but for this plant it probably would have been a good idea.

Two other blue spruce selections with superior qualities of have earned the Iseli name: 'Iseli Fastigiate' and 'Iseli Foxtail'. 'Fastigiate' is described in the catalogue as a "sentinel" that looks "like a fat, steel blue cigar" while 'Foxtail', as an open pyramidal form with distinctive blue needles that become shorter in length as they grow closer to the tip of the shoots. According to the late J. C. Raulston, 'Foxtail' is also the most heat tolerant of all the spruces he studied.

The only plant ever patented by Iseli Nursery is *Juniperus horizontalis* 'Mother Lode'. André says that his brother told him lightning struck a juniper (*Juniperus horizontalis* 'Wiltoni') in his garden in 1982 and split the original plant in half. This act of nature turned one half of the plant gold and gave rise to the name, 'Mother Lode'.

The unique dwarf conifer *Picea glauca* 'Jean's Dilly,' was named in tribute to his late brother. The definition of the English word "dilly" means someone or something that is outstanding or remarkable. This spruce possesses a unique characteristic of thin short needles arranged in a distinctive twist at the end of the shoots, so André called it a "dilly", a term equally accurate in describing his much-missed brother.

André continues to dream about producing wonderful plants. One of his hopes is to graft the leaf of the dissected Japanese maple ('Red Dragon') on to the paperbark maple, *Acer griseum*. Another wish is to have tissue culture methods for propagating conifers perfected. His visions generate fantastic grafted plant combinations and large topiaries, which he confesses are probably the "manifestations of a frustrated artist". According to Iseli, he never had so much fun as working at his nursery, both running the business and creating the plants. He also states he never worked with nicer people and suggests, "The closer people work with the earth, the nicer they are." Recently, Iseli Nursery was merged under the International Garden Products umbrella, combining Iseli's extraordinary conifers with a broad range of other nursery offerings. No longer involved in the day to day nursery operations, André may choose yet another fascinating path for his life's most stimulating journey. Regardless, the world of horticulture will continue to benefit as long as Andrè Iseli continues to dream.

References

Iseli, André. "An Artistic Manifestation." *American Nurseryman* August 15, 1991:38-42.
Iseli Nursery Plant Catalogues

Acknowledgment

André Iseli

Photograph by Dean Copeland.

TINA JAMES

Tina James

Oenothera glazioviana 'Tina James'

Tina Nield refers to her namesake primrose as "magic", and to all who know the flower, this description is perfect. In the summertime at dusk, it is possible, even with the naked eye, to watch the yellow flower petals unfurl one after the other, as though they were part of an enchanted kingdom. Audiences in lawn chairs sit before the evening primroses and excitedly await the evening's entertaining display. Fortunate are those who witness the astounding performance of *Oenothera glazioviana* 'Tina James'.

This fascinating plant is better known in Europe than in the United States even though it is hybrid of a North American evening primrose. Nield explains it must have traveled to Europe and returned to this country during the early 1700's, when many plant exchanges were being made between the old world and the new.

The primrose may have found its way back to North America with German immigrants. During the early 1980's, on her weekly visit to purchase goat's milk at a farm in the German community of Frizzellburg, Maryland, Tina "rediscovered" the magic flower. One evening, about sunset, she was enjoying a chat across the fence with the farm's owners, Esther and Ray Arrington. All at once, the fields around them lit up with beautiful yellow flowers spinning open. The Arringtons hardly noticed this astounding event, but Tina was enthralled. Esther could not tell Tina the name or source of the plants, but then and there she dug one and gave it to her.

Tina has enjoyed the magic primroses in her own garden ever since, and has distributed seeds to seed companies, plant society seed exchanges, and public gardens. In recognition of her rediscovery of the plant, Southern Exposure Seed Exchange named the plant in her honor. They chose her professional name, Tina James, which she used as a host of an organic gardening show on Maryland public television.

Tina Nield grew up in a town near Annapolis on Maryland's Eastern Shore. Her parents instilled in her the beauty of nature that she has always enjoyed and continues to share. After obtaining her degree in English from Allegheny College in Meadville, Pennsylvania in 1974, she honed her communication skills while working at Maryland Public Television. There Tina met Jean Worthley, who appeared as "Miss Jean" on a popular children's nature show called Hodge Podge Lodge. It was Worthley who asked Nield to host a series on organic gardening that Tina developed into "Good Earth Garden". In her television persona, Tina became "Aunt Tina", and adopted the name James.

The magic primrose became another bond between the two women. Part of Tina's delight in the plant has always come from sharing it with friends through a tradition of hosting summer evening "viewing" parties for the magic primrose. Among the guests invited were Jean and her botanist-husband, Elmer. It turned out that they had previously been treated to a magic primrose performance at the farm of friends in Pullman, West Virginia, but no one there knew the flower's name. The Worthley's sent samples of the plant to Warren Wagner, a leading authority on primroses at the Missouri Botanical Garden. He responded that the plant "probably originated in a garden in Europe through hybridization between commonly cultivated North American species such as *O. hookeri* (now known as *O. elata*) and *O. biennis*, a very common weed in eastern North America. *Oenothera glazioviana* was known to be in the horticultural trade by 1860. It is now naturalized nearly throughout the world.

O. galzioviana is a biennial and prefers a sunny location. It grows into a rosette similar to a dandelion its first summer, and into a 2'-5' bushy plant the second year when the flowers appear. The slightly fragrant yellow flowers open in stages, the first being the mature flowers on the outside ring. Individual plants can produce as many as one hundred flowers on a single evening and can continue to bloom each night for many weeks.

Tina and her husband George Beneman, live in Reisterstown, Maryland, where her garden continues to produce wonderful fruits, flowers and herbs. Although Tina Nield no longer appears on TV, she remains an enthusiastic communicator. Her books include *Gardening from the Heart*, (1986), and *Cooking with Herbs*, (1999). In 1996 she wrote the delightful A *Light in the Night: The Story of the Magic Primrose*. "Aunt Tina" still enjoys teaching children about nature and conducts a summertime camp program at her Maryland home. There is no doubt she shares the story of the magic primrose with her campers.

At present, Tina is exploring herbal medicines and holographic repatterning, but she will always have a special connection to the flower that brings smiles to the faces of all who witness Mother Nature at her best.

References

James, Tina. A *Light in the Night: The Story of the Magic Primrose*. Reisterstown: Gardening from the Heart, 1996.
Robson, Nancy Taylor. "A coming-out Party". *The Sun*. Sunday, September 8, 1996: 7K.

Acknowledgments

Tina James
Jean Worthley

Photogrph by George R. Beneman.

JOSEPH KASSAB

Joseph Kassab

Ilex x 'Doctor Kassab'

Joseph Kassab's vocation was practicing medicine, but his avocation was gardening. He was a keen holly enthusiast and a long time member and trustee of the Holly Society of America. According to his wife Betty, Kassab considered the naming of *Ilex* x 'Doctor Kassab' to be his most significant honor and recognition.

The plant that became the 'Doctor Kassab' holly appeared as part of a large order of seedling Chinese hollies (*Ilex cornuta*) which Kassab purchased in 1948 from Davenport Nurseries in Pennsylvania. As the plants matured, he noticed that one differed from the others by having small, pointed, dark green leaves with only two spines on each side. The plant was a female and produced round red berries that persisted throughout the fall and winter. After 20 years the plant became a conical, 25'-tall shrub with a 10' spread of horizontal branches.

Considering the possibility it was a new holly altogether, he rooted cuttings and sent them in 1965 to the National Arboretum, where Gene Eisenbeiss and Ted Dudley were conducting holly research and promoting hollies as garden plants. They tested Kassab's holly and declared that it was a new hybrid, probably *Ilex aquifolium* x *Ilex cornuta*, and asked Joe Kassab what he wished to name it. A fellow holly enthusiast and Kassab's close friend, Sam Souder, insisted that it should be named 'Doctor Kassab.'

The Philadelphia area was always home to Joseph Kassab. He grew up in Wallingford, Pennsylvania, only two doors down the road from the house where Betty lives today. As a boy he worked in the garden of his neighbor, Edwin Rosenbluth, a rosarian and chemist whose specialty was finding pesticides and fungicides for roses. Rosenbluth paid Kassab twenty-five cents a day to help clear his garden of spent rose petals, but the true reward was the lifelong love for gardening given to the young man.

Later, the Rosenbluth house came up for sale, and the Kassab family purchased it. For more than one reason it was a momentous time the family would never forget. The day after they bought their wonderful new home with its rose garden, news of the "day that will live in infamy," the attack on Pearl Harbor, shocked the world. Soon after, Joseph Kassab, who had graduated from LaFayette College in Easton, Pennsylvania and from Hahnemann Medical School (today Allegheny Health Systems) joined the military and served as a doctor in the Pacific. After the war he returned to live in Wallingford and began practicing medicine as a general surgeon in Philadelphia. He joined his family in the house where he had worked as a boy and lived there for the rest of his life. Joseph Kassab died in 1991 at the age of 82.

Betty and Joseph Kassab were married in 1953. The couple met at a hospital where he practiced and where she was an x-ray technician. She remembers with amusement that while they were dating, she received a phone call from one of Kassab's former girl friends who asked if Betty "was willing to play second fiddle to a rose." Despite her suitor's reputation for putting plants above all else, they married and began gardening and housekeeping at his parents' home.

From roses to hollies, Kassab worked passionately with plants. During the war, whenever he had the chance, he collected seeds to plant in his Pennsylvania garden when he returned home. Betty recalls that few grew; however, the doctor's love for new and different plants was clearly demonstrated. Later, as he and Betty gardened together, their appetites for plants increased, and they built a small greenhouse. In 1972, they added a facility for propagation, grew more plants, especially hollies, and began to sell a few as well. For 23 years, with their friend Souder, they sold hollies at the Philadelphia Flower Show. In 1973, at their show booth, they first offered Ilex x 'Doctor Kassab.' Since that time it has been propagated by many nurseries and become a mainstream garden plant.

Today the Kassab's daughter, Eleanor Ford, with her husband and two daughters, lives with Betty. Eleanor continues to work in the same greenhouse her parents built. Along with the popular holly named for her father, she grows a number of other outstanding plants and sells to the general public.

Gardeners who grow Kassab's holly should be pleased to know they have a plant named for a man who was just as popular as the plant that bears his name. Fred Galle, the late Director of Horticulture at Callaway Gardens, remembered him as a captivating storyteller with amazing recall who delighted in amusing his audiences with tales about his life and his plants, especially about his discovery of the holly. He gave pleasure to many gardeners, as does his namesake plant.

Reference

Galle, Fred. Hollies. Portland: Timber Press, 1997.

Acknowledgments

Elizabeth Kassab
John Ruter

Photograph courtesy of Elizabeth Kassab.

HELLA LACY

Hella Lacy

Aster 'Hella Lacy'

Anyone settling in for a relaxing session of arm-chair gardening is sure to find midst the beckoning stack of catalogues, books, and magazines numerous compositions by one of America's most popular garden writers, Allen Lacy. In his countless articles and columns, and in the eleven books he authored or edited, Lacy's engaging prose and candid opinions have entertained readers and provided many vicarious gardening experiences.

Although Lacy has enjoyed gardening since his boyhood in Dallas, Texas, his formal education had little to do with horticulture. He majored in English literature at Duke University where he earned a Bachelor of Arts degree in 1956. After briefly attending divinity school at Vanderbilt University, he returned to Duke and received a doctorate in religion in 1962. He held teaching positions at several institutions before joining the philosophy faculty at Richard Stockton College of New Jersey in Linwood in 1971.

During the years he was teaching philosophy, he began to pen his thoughts about gardening and, as his writing interests turned in that direction, he added an occasional course in ornamental horticulture to his teaching schedule. Allen will tell you, however, that his real gardening experiences come from working with his wife, Hella, on the quarter-acre of land they share in Linwood. Before settling in suburban southern New Jersey, Lacy's career took the family to many different states, including Tennessee, North Carolina, South Carolina, Virginia, and Michigan, and, yet, for every home they created a garden.

Lacy readily admits that Hella is the real gardener, the one who prunes, weeds, and tends to the garden's daily needs, while he, on the other hand, writes about what they have accomplished. One of their sons once observed that his dad "gardens at the computer." Allen's writing, however, is simply the more public part of his participation. Both Hella and he enjoy plants and collect them avidly. Whenever the garden's ownership is discussed there is no doubt it belongs to Hella and Allen together.

Hella Lacy was born in Berlin in 1937, when Germany was embarking on a tragic period in its history. There was little gardening for her to enjoy as a child. Her father, Bernhard Hermann Goethert, was an aeronautical engineer and an expert in wind tunnels. At the end of World War II he was captured by the Allies as one of a group of German rocket scientists and taken to Ohio in 1946. Hella, her mother, and three brothers followed him two years later. In 1950, the family moved to Manchester, Tennessee, where Goethert worked for the Arnold Engineering Development Corporation in Tullahoma. Subsequently, in the same town, he founded the University of Tennessee Space Institute and was its dean for many years.

Hella's dream was to become a nurse. She enrolled in Vanderbilt University's School of Nursing during the time Allen was attending the divinity school. Lacy first saw Hella one February morning and thought "she was the most beautiful woman I had ever seen"--and has not changed his mind since. Their first date was Valentine's Day, and they were married the following Thanksgiving. The November holiday became even more special to them when their first son, Paul, was born the following year, on Thanksgiving, which fell on November 26. Even more coincidentally, their second son, Michael, was born three years later, also on November 26. Hella quickly became the manager of a busy household.

Lacy named an exceptional New England aster in tribute to his wife. The flower first caught his attention when he saw it in his neighborhood in Linwood, where they moved in 1972. Although it was quite common, no one seemed to know anything about it. It grew 3-4' tall and produced violet-blue flowers with bright yellow centers. Lacy guessed it might be a new variety useful to gardeners. His suspicions were confirmed by horticulturists at White Flower Farm and by André Viette, whose nursery "set it loose in the American world of horticulture." When Viette asked him to name the plant for introduction, Lacy thought immediately of Hella.

Once the plant was introduced, Lacy seriously began to research its background. He traced the origins to the early 1900s and to the principal of Linwood's Belhaven School, a man who apparently was interested in gardening. The principal was a boarder in the home that now belongs to Lacy's neighbors, and Lacy believes the original aster was probably planted by the educator in that garden.

Hella has experienced both the good and bad in her celebrity status. Gardening friends often agree that 'Hella' is a beautiful flower while also suggesting that she benefits from "chopping back" each summer. In spite of the joking, the two Hellas are both worthy of praise. In one of his most popular books, *The Garden in Autumn*, Lacy lauds *Aster* 'Hella Lacy' and reveals the following: "When I first clapped eyes on it in a front yard just down the block, I knew it was classy." Lucky for gardeners, Allen Lacy is quick to recognize exceptional beauty.

References

Lacy, Allen. *The Garden in Autumn*. New York: The Atlantic Monthly Press, 1990.

Pardue, Leonard. "How Does Your Garden Grow? Allen Lacy". *Duke Magazine* July-August 1994: 35-37.

Acknowledgments
Allen Lacy
Mildred Pinnell
Mark Viette

Photograph courtesy of Allen Lacy.

MICHAEL LINDSEY

Michael Lindsey

Calycanthus floridus 'Michael Lindsey'

Tracy Cochrane began work at Holbrook Farm in Fletcher, North Carolina, when she was 16 years old and worked there the next 14 years. When she married Craig Lindsey in 1988, the couple moved into a cottage at the nursery. They were still living at the nursery when their son, Michael Thomas Lindsey, was born on October 8, 1991. Not long after his birth, they received a most extraordinary baby gift.

Each spring for many years, professors Michael Dirr and Allan Armitage took a group of horticulture students from the University of Georgia on a trip to Asheville, North Carolina to tour the gardens at Biltmore House as well as nurseries and private gardens along the way. In the spring of 1991, during a visit to Holbrook Farm, Dirr caught sight of a striking sweet shrub (*Calycanthus floridus*), growing near Craig and Tracy's cottage.

Allen Bush, the owner of Holbrook Farm, had no idea where the plant originated and knew it only as a no-name cultivar from a local outlet. But Dirr claimed it was special and noted it had exceptionally lustrous dark green leaves plus deliciously fragrant reddish brown flowers, a winning combination for sweet shrubs. Most sweet shrubs exhibit either fragrant flowers or good foliage color, but seldom both. This plant had it all. Additionally, it becomes a dense, compact plant with a mature height of 6' to 8' and in the fall its foliage is golden yellow.

Tracy remembers that Bush took Dirr's evaluation to heart, and she was put to work rooting calycanthus cuttings. Even more distinctly, she remembers that she was pregnant. About the time her baby was due, she produced a calycanthus crop ready to be sold. Needing a name for his new plant, Bush celebrated the birth of Craig and Tracy's little boy by naming the plant in honor of their son. *Calycanthus floridus* 'Michael Lindsey' was introduced by Holbrook Farm Nursery and first sold in 1993.

Even as a baby, Michael enjoyed his namesake plant. In the spring his parents opened his nursery window to allow the fragrance to fill his room. In 1995, when Bush closed Holbrook Farm and the Lindseys moved to Asheville, one of young Michael's sweet shrubs also went along and was planted beside the front entrance walk to their new home. The youngster continues to delight in the plant, and its place along the walkway makes it convenient for introducing "the other Michael Lindsey" to those who pass. Michael also proudly possesses his own copy of the 5th edition of Dirr's *Manual of Woody Landscape Plants* with its dog-eared page 167, the page where his sweet shrub is described.

The red-haired and freckle-faced young man with sparkling blue eyes has a wonderful sense of humor, an insatiable curiosity, and a love for reading. In addition to attending elementary school in Asheville, Michael Lindsey is also enrolled in Sanford University's online program for gifted youth, which concentrates on math and computer science. His extracurricular activities include playing soccer year round. Plants and gardening have a place in his life, too. Three times each week he accompanies Tracy to the garden center where she works and assists customers and staff. He is also an active participant in the Lindseys' garden at home. When his parents inquire what he wants to plant, he unwaveringly chooses pumpkins and things with orange flowers, perfect selections for a bright and energetic youngster with red hair.

Having his own namesake plant almost since birth has surely given young Michael Lindsey an appreciation for plants and gardening that he will carry with him all his life. And, thanks to Allen Bush, the beauty of *Calycanthus floridus* 'Michael Lindsey' will bring joy and pleasure to every gardener who plants it.

Reference
Dirr, Michael A. *Manual of Woody Landscape Plants*.
5th edition. Champaign: Stipes Publishing, 1998.

Acknowledgments
Allen Bush
Tracy Lindsey

Photograph courtesy of Tracy Lindsey.

CAROL MACKIE

Carol Mackie

Daphne x *burkwoodii* 'Carol Mackie'

Carol Mackie's friends describe her as "delightful, special, and popular," words often duplicated when gardeners refer to the plant that bears her name, *Daphne* x *burkwoodii* 'Carol Mackie.' Carol discovered the plant in her New Jersey garden in 1962 and it has become one of the most desirable of all shrubs. The small, dark green leaves are handsomely edged in a creamy white border, and in early summer, its rose-pink buds unfold to make a truly stunning display of fragrant pale-pink flowers. A distinctive, densely mounded form growing to a height of 3'–4', the 'Carol Mackie' daphne is easily included in residential gardens. It is, indeed, a delightful, special, and popular garden plant.

That Mackie noticed the sport on her *Daphne* x *burkwoodii* is not surprising. Her friends also describe her as "a splendid amateur horticulturist." She learned horticulture from being a gardener, a passion she developed extensively after she was married and living on a farm.

Carolyn Bartow Sherwood was born on December 30, 1908, the younger of two daughters, and grew up in Englewood, New Jersey. She attended Dwight School, a private girls' school, and earned a bachelor's degree in art from Smith College in 1932.

121

Returning to Englewood after graduation, she taught algebra and geometry at Dwight until she married David Ives Mackie on April 30, 1937. The couple continued to live in Englewood while David commuted to New York City to practice law. After several years David became general counsel for the Delaware, Lackawanna, and Western Railroad, and they moved to the country near Far Hills, New Jersey, a stop on the DL&W.

Wing Feather Farm became the Mackies' new home where they raised their two sons, David III and Arthur, and numerous animals. While chickens, geese, turkeys, Hampshire sheep, pigs, and a horse for the boys to ride became residents, there was always plenty of room for gardening on the farm and Carol soon began to plant her first flower beds

Carol joined the Garden Club of Short Hills and in a short time became active with The Garden Club of America. Ultimately she served as First Vice President, and with her knowledge of horticulture, colorful storytelling, and engaging sense of humor she became a popular speaker. During the years she worked with GCA she traveled extensively to lecture about horticulture.

In addition to her formal offices, Mackie actively participated with a group of GCA friends who referred to themselves as "the Rares," or the Rare Plant Committee. The common bond of this group was their singular love of unusual plants: learning about them, looking for them, growing them, and sharing them. They visited one another's homes to discuss their plant experiences and traveled together to many parts of the world to find their specimens. Carol's family remembers how she returned home from her horticulture safaris with her newfound treasures, albeit roadside cuttings, stuck inside her pockets and purse. Innocently she revealed them and remarked that "God put them there." As one of "the Rares," Carol Mackie furthered her horticultural knowledge and increased her collection of exotic plants.

In 1954, when their boys were away at school, Carol and David moved to a smaller home near Far Hills. According to their neighbor, Mrs. Russell Fossbinder, it was not the house, but the 20 acres of empty pasture and the close proximity of her horse farm with its abundant source of manure, that caused the Mackies to purchase the property. It wasn't long before Carol's farm developed into a thriving, densely planted garden. The two neighbors jokingly compared their farms: Fossbinder's was known as "Clearfield," and the Mackies' was known as "Fullfield."

Recurring back problems caused Carol to set about making plans for a more carefree garden at her new home. She planted mostly shrubs and trees, and this decision eventually led to her discovery of the special daphne. Organizing the "Fullfield" plant collection into a scheme of 34 island gardens that ultimately included about 300 different species, she named most of the islands for their dominant plant, but some were descriptive, such as the Flagpole Island, the Stone Island, the Anniversary Islands, and the Gas Tank Island. On the Laburnum Island she planted three *Daphne* x *burkwoodii*.

One of the Laburnum Island daphnes issued the variegated sport that caught Carol's attention. She made cuttings of the unusual branch and gave a couple to the late Don Smith at Watnong Nursery. Smith propagated Mackie's discovery and decided to name it for her. He sent the registration information to Donald Huttleston of Longwood Gardens who published it in *Arnoldia*, the journal of the Arnold Arboretum, in 1970. The 'Carol Mackie' daphne is somewhat difficult to propagate, but nurseries have succeeded in making it available and it has become a favorite with gardeners. Its appearance in the Wayside Gardens catalogue in 1989, a recognition thought by some to be the horticultural equal to Hollywood's Academy Award, magnified its popularity.

By the time *Daphne* x *burkwoodii* 'Carol Mackie' was being sold in the East, Carol had moved to California. David tragically died following heart surgery in 1966, and the following year Carol visited her college roommate in Rancho Santa Fe. She immediately fell in love with the area and in 1967 moved there to begin a new life. Because the California climate was not suited for growing daphnes, Carol's gardening attention

123

was directed to other plant types, and she was unaware the plant she discovered had been named for her. She finally learned about her namesake plant from gardening friends back east who had seen it for sale.

In Rancho Santa Fe, Mackie steered her gardening passion in new directions and created a hillside of succulents. Visiting friends found her new garden quite a contrast to the one she had developed in New Jersey, but equally wonderful. Guests were delighted by her amusing "wild animal park," an artfully planted collection of succulents in animal-shaped pots. And, no one was ever allowed to depart her garden without a sample succulent.

In 1971, Carol Mackie met Roger Brett and they were married in January 1972. After eight happy years, Roger died from cancer. Several years later Carol moved to an apartment and then to a retirement home in Carlsbad, where she died April 24, 1999. The Quail Botanical Garden in Encinitas was chosen as the site for her memorial service. It was a place Carol loved; she had served on its board while she lived in California.

Carol Mackie Brett was an outstanding gardener and a most captivating woman. She found the perfect plant to bear her name.

References

Bruckel, Dennis. "Propagating 'Carol Mackie' is Well Worth the Effort." *American Nurseryman* August 15, 1989: 62-63.

Mackie, Carolyn Sherwood. "My Garden: Yearlong Beauty from Trees and Shrubs." *Flower Grower* September, 1959.

Mackie, Carolyn S. "Some Enduring Favorites." *The Garden Journal, The New York Botanical Garden* November-December 1964: 210-313.

Mackie, Carolyn S. "This is Your Life-Carolyn Sherwood Mackie Brett." Paper delivered to Rancho Santa Fe Book Club May 27, 1986.

Acknowledgments
John Elsley
Mrs. Russell Fossbinder
Beth Gainer
Mary Homans
Hilda King
Carol and David Mackie, Jr.
Mrs. Prentice Talmage, Jr.

Photograph courtesy of Carol Mackie (Mrs. David, Jr.).

DOROTHY METHENY

Dorothy Metheny

Erica x *watsonii* 'Dorothy Metheny'

Dorothy Metheny's love for gardening and her passion for heathers led her to become an authority on both heaths and heathers. She studied them intensely and in 1991, just before she turned 90 years old, Dee, (as she was known to her friends), published the culmination of her life's work, *Hardy Heather Species*, a compilation of her descriptions, drawings, and information about their origins, habits, and attributes. The book includes the five genera defined by the International Registration Authority for Heather Cultivar Names: *Andromeda*, *Bruckenthalia*, *Calluna*, *Daboecia*, and *Erica* plus two North American genera in the heather family: the mountain heath, *Phyllodoce*; and mountain heather, *Cassiope*. Although the book sounds complex and terribly academic, it is, according to the author, "a book for gardeners by a gardener."

That Dorothy Metheny became such a respected and knowledgeable gardener and writer was not forecast in her early years. The youngest of three children, Dorothy was born in Chicago on September 25, 1901, and grew up there. She attended Nicholas Senn High School, where her athletic accomplishments led her to be chosen as the sports reporter for the student newspaper, a most uncommon job for a female student in 1919. Although the family's home was surrounded by a yard, neither her businessman father, Frank Macomber, nor her mother, a home-maker, were particularly keen about gardening. Dorothy Metheny did not start gardening until she moved to Seattle, Washington, but that passion became her second career.

In 1923, Dorothy received her B.A. degree in psychology from Wellesley College (she noted that her degree would be "physi-ology" when compared with today's definition of psychology). In 1926 she married David Metheny, a resident at the Mayo Clinic, and the couple moved to Rochester, Minnesota. Four years later, David began his medical practice in Seattle, and they moved to the hillside home where Dorothy lived and gardened until her death on March 2, 2000, at the age of 98. David always encour-aged Dee's gardening efforts and was her official photographer until he died in 1972.

The Methenys had four children, Frank, Sterrett, David, and Kate. As the children were growing up, the garden was mainly a playground, and the fruit trees were used for climbing. While raising her children, Metheny was involved in civic affairs, serv-ing as president of Planned Parenthood of Seattle and actively participating in the University Unitarian Church. When the youngest child, Kate, was around 12 years old, her mother replaced the playground with a heather garden. Infatuated by a gift of a heather called 'Darley Dale', Dee announced to her family that heathers are "the ideal plants for the garden." In the late 1950's, Dee Metheny began her adventure with her chosen plants. In time, more than 200 species of heathers shared her beautiful garden.

Metheny was a self-taught gardener, a heather connoisseur, and an active member of the North American Rock Garden Society. When she decided to specialize in heathers, she stud-ied them persistently and kept meticulous records. She used a microscope to observe each new heather and made detailed drawings. She found the process exhilarating, and delighted in sharing her knowledge and ideas with others. To encourage this exchange among heather enthusiasts, she and six other heather aficionados met in Vancouver, British Columbia in 1977 and created the North American Heather Society.

The quarterly publication of the NAHS is called *Heather News*. Dorothy Metheny was its editor for 10 years and her descriptions and drawings, which later were incorporated into her book, first appeared in its pages. She also wrote for the year book of the Heather Society (UK) and served as its Vice President from 1969 until her death. It was her association with the British society that led to the heather that bears her name.

Erica x *watsonii* 'Dorothy Metheny' was discovered on Harland Moor, Dorset, England, in September, 1979, by Heather Society members on an afternoon's walk during their annual conference. Major General P.G. Turpin of West Clandon, Guildford, Surrey, who later became the chairman of the society, registered the plant's name in 1987 as 'Dorothy Metheny'. In her book Metheny describes E. x *watsonii* as a "group of natural hybrid cultivars" (E. *ciliaris* x E. *tetralix*) with flowers which "resemble the bottle-shape bells of *ciliaris*...". In the book, *Handy Guide to Heathers*, written for the Heather Society by David and Anne Small, 'Dorothy Metheny' is described as having pale lilac flowers deepening with age and bright green foliage tipped yellow in spring.

Having this handsome heather named for this remarkable woman was a well-earned recognition. When Dee Metheny heard her namesake plant described as having a "much better garden constitution" compared to other hearhers, she smiled. Dorothy Metheny lived a full and rich life and will be remembered by lovers of this wonderful group of plants.

References

Metheny, Dorothy M. *Hardy Heather Species*. Seaside: Frontier Publishing, 1991.

Small, Ann and David Small. *Handy Guide to Heathers*. The Heather Society, UK, 1998-99.

Acknowledgments
Ellen Norris
Kate Metheny Baldwin
David Small

Photograph courtesy of Kate Baldwin and the North American Heather Society.

FRANK N. MEYER

Frank N. Meyer

Citrus x limonia 'Meyer'
(*Citrus x meyeri*)

On the dessert menu of exclusive restaurants, one of the selections may well be Meyer Lemon ice cream, a happy discovery for all diners, even those who have no idea of the history they are savoring. The ice cream's particular lemon flavoring comes from a plant collected by a little known but most remarkable man, plant explorer Frank N. Meyer. Meyer was sent to Asia in the early 1900s by the Department of Agriculture to search for crops suitable for the United States, and he made four quite amazing expeditions. The Meyer lemon is only one of his approximately 2,500 plant introductions.

Meyer was born in Holland on November 29, 1875, and emigrated to the United States in 1901. His career goals were formed early: at the end of the sixth grade, he announced to his parents that he planned to study plants and be a world traveler.

He left school at the age of 14 to work as a gardener at the Amsterdam Botanical Garden. There he attracted the attention of the eminent Dutch botanist, his first employer and lifelong mentor, Hugo De Vries. Recognizing Meyer's innate abilities and love for learning, De Vries encouraged him to take courses in languages and physics and to pursue studies at the University of Gronigen. When Meyer completed his studies, he began his first exploration trip. Frank Meyer was a fitness enthusiast long before it was fashionable, and on this first trip he walked across the European continent and over the Alps into Italy.

For his next adventure, he decided to travel to the United States. To secure funds for his passage he spent a year working in commercial nurseries near London. Once he was in the U.S., the zealous Meyer found his training in Amsterdam, his passion for plants, and his physical stamina were all qualities that would serve him well in the years to come.

Plant exploration was not a new occupation in the early 20th century. Private individuals and botanical gardens had been searching for new species around the globe for many years. However, Frank Meyer was a unique plant explorer in that he came to be employed by a government agency to search for plants to benefit agriculture. His position was the legacy of another extraordinary man, David Fairchild.

Fairchild, one of America's most notable botanists, worked for the United States Department of Agriculture. Highly respected in his profession, he persuaded Congress to create the Office of Foreign Seed and Plant Introduction in the USDA. In 1898, Fairchild became its first chief and immediately suggested that the government send an explorer to Asia with the purpose of collecting plants useful for agriculture. As Fairchild began to search for someone to do the job, he was told about Frank Meyer, then an employee at the Missouri Botanical Garden. In July 1905, Fairchild met Meyer and knew he had found the perfect man for the task. Meyer left for China in August that same year promising, "to skim the earth in search of good things for man."

Exploring the Far East in 1905 was a daunting undertaking, but Meyer allowed no obstacle to stand in his way of collecting plants for the USDA. With the constant travel on foot, the weather, the politics, and the Spartan conditions, difficulties and hardships were commonplace. All four of his expeditions between 1905 and 1918, were incredibly punishing and often life-threatening. Yet, it would be difficult to tell the story of a plant explorer who loved his occupation more. "I can hardly believe," he wrote to his parents, "I got such a beautiful job." And during those years, Meyer found time to become a U.S. citizen.

Meyer's first expedition took him on a three-year odyssey to China, Manchuria, and Korea. It was during this trip that he first described an especially ornamental lemon plant. Although Meyer failed to make note of its origin, he probably purchased the plant from a nursery in Fentai near Peking. According to his records, on the same day at that nursery, he purchased a lilac, later to be named *Syringa meyeri*.

Meyer lemon is known as *Citrus x limonia* 'Meyer' (also, *citrus x meyeri*). It is not a true lemon, but is likely a hybrid between *Citrus limon*, the true lemon and *C. Reticulata*, the mandarin orange. The fruit is somewhat larger, much juicier, and more cold tolerant than true lemons, but because of its susceptibility to shipping damage, it was never widely adopted by the citrus industry. It has been successful in local markets, however, and has proven useful for juice processing and flavoring, such as in ice cream . It is also a popular ornamental pot plant, especially in California.

In July 1906 Meyer collected grass seeds in northern Korea and included the following notation in his records: "A perennial grass growing but a few inches high, well adapted for lawn purposes. Needs mowing, in all probability, but once or twice a year and requires very little water.... There were donkeys continually browsing upon this grass, but it was one green velvet turf and will be excellent for golf links, lawns, etc." The grass came to be known as zoysia grass (*Zoysia japonica*) and because Meyer first introduced it to the United States, the USDA chose to honor him by giving his name to a zoysia variety, although the particular cultivar chosen was actually a selection from seeds collected in Korea in the 1930s. Meyer zoysia is the most popular of the zoysia grasses for the Midwest, East, and South.

During his next three trips to Asia, Meyer continued to collect plants that were to become highly successful in both agriculture and ornamental horticulture. Of his 2, 500 introductions, many bear his name, such as *Juniperus squamata* 'Meyeri' (Meyer juniper), *Picea meyeri* (Meyer spruce), *Prunus x meyeri* (Korean cherry), and *Syringa meyeri* (dwarf lilac). Other Meyer ornamental introductions include *Diospyros kaki* (Chinese persimmon), *Pyrus calleryana* (Callery Pear), *Ulmus parvifolia* (Chinese elm), and, *Ulmus pumila* (Siberian elm), as well as many useful varieties of soybeans, alfalfa, and barley.

Having such a large number of successful introductions to his credit is largely due to his method of collecting plants. Instead of digging entire plants, Meyer sent back seeds and unrooted cuttings that resulted in improved propagation once in the United States. Many of Meyer's plants were shared with other horticultural institutions, such as the Arnold Arboretum, and thereby were assured of even greater dissemination.

Meyer departed for his fourth expedition in August 1916. On May 31, 1918, under highly mysterious circumstances, he disappeared from a Japanese river boat, *Feng Yang Maru*, on the Yangtze River. His body was later recovered and buried in the Bubbling Well Protestant Cemetery in Shanghai. To this day, his death remains a mystery.

Meyer's will included a bequest of $1,000 to his colleagues in Washington and was used to establish the Meyer Memorial Medal for excellence in the field of plant introduction. The inscription on the medal is written in Chinese characters and reads, "In the glorious luxuriance of the thousand plants he takes delight," a fitting tribute to the explorer whose life the award commemorates. The first Meyer Medal was presented in 1920 to Barbour Lathrop, the man who inspired David Fairchild to create the Office of Foreign Seed and Plant Introduction. Fairchild himself, the man who so believed in Meyer's ability, received the medal in 1939. Today, the award is administered by the Crop Science Society of America.

At the time of Meyer's death, many tributes were written to celebrate his extraordinary life and his numerous gifts to American horticulture and agriculture. As the years have passed, these words of tribute have faded from public memory, but Frank Meyer's plant introductions remain living reminders of this remarkable man.

Reference

Cunningham, Isabel Shipley. *Frank N. Meyer, Plant Hunter in Asia*. Ames: Iowa State University Press, 1984.

Acknowledgments

Isabel Shipley Cunningham
Tom Foley
Sara Lee
Frank Linton

Photograph courtesy of National Agricultural Library, Document Delivery Services Branch, Beltsville, MD.

MONTROSE
NURSERY

Nancy Goodwin

Heuchera 'Montrose Ruby'

Nancy Goodwin's dream was to transform the landscape at her home, Montrose, into the most wonderful garden possible. In pursuit of her dream, this energetic and talented woman also created an excellent nursery that produced an outstanding coral bell called *Heuchera* 'Montrose Ruby.' According to Nancy, the plant fortuitously resulted from "a cross made by the bees, not by me," but because of her wonderful discovery, both her distinguished nursery and stunning garden are remembered.

The Durham, North Carolina, native dreamed of finding a home that provided gracious spaces for each of her two passions: gardening and teaching music. In 1977 she and her husband, Craufurd, purchased a lovely old house called Montrose on property first developed in the 1820s in the historic village of Hillsborough, North Carolina.

William Alexander and Susan Washington Graham named the property Montrose in the mid-1840s in honor of their ancestral hometown in Scotland. It remained in the Graham family for three generations. Fire destroyed the original house, and the house on the property today is the third built there; however, some of the original auxiliary buildings still stand. One of these was the law office of Mr. Graham who later served as governor of North Carolina from 1845 until 1849.

When Nancy Goodwin began working in the garden at Montrose, she found trees dating from the time of the original Graham residency. A wonderful serpentine border of boxwoods also survived from the 1920s. While Nancy still lived in Durham, propagating boxwoods had become an interest of hers, and she could not resist rooting cuttings from the ones at Montrose. Another plant interest from her Durham days was hardy cyclamen, a plant she had learned to propagate from seed. Heat-tolerant primroses were also on her list of horticultural fascinations.

Within a year of moving to Montrose, Nancy had a number of plants in production and was making some of them available. She also continued to develop her garden. As word of her accomplishments spread, visitors came, and she had many requests for plants. After careful thought and planning, she increased her production, especially her cyclamen, and in 1984 opened Montrose Nursery as a mail-order business. Plant enthusiasts quickly realized the unique nature and outstanding quality of Nancy Goodwin's plants.

Nancy ran the nursery alone for two years, all the while continuing to teach music, but the demand for Montrose plants grew to the point she needed to hire help. She added staff and increased her plant inventory, both in numbers and species. Her plant list now included many perennials not readily available at that time, and Montrose became widely recognized for its unusual offerings.

Montrose plants are propagated from seed, and it was seed propagation that gave rise to the discovery of the Montrose coral bell. Each year seeds from known coral bells were routinely collected and planted in flats. In the late 1980s, one flat of new seedlings produced some plants with remarkable, dark purple leaves beautifully enhanced by a silver mottling. Recognizing the unique appearance of the plant, Nancy named this new cultivar *Heuchera* 'Montrose Ruby.' It was described as, "the result of a happy marriage of *H.* 'Palace Purple' and *H.* 'Dale's Strain.'" in the Montrose catalogue. In the nursery's record of observations the entries for 'Montrose Ruby' suggest that its tiny, cream-colored spring flowers are insignificant, but its leaves retain their deep purple color throughout the summer. The first year it was offered, the new plant sold out.

Customer demands for 'Montrose Ruby' required the nursery to grow large numbers of plants. However, in 1993, most of the supply died as the result of over watering. Every surviving healthy plant was mailed, and money for unfilled orders was returned. As a result, not a single 'Montrose Ruby' remained at the nursery. Potential disaster loomed, for there would be no more namesake coral bells if there were no source for seed. Fortunately, the saying, "The best way to save a plant is to share it," proved to be true. Nancy had given her plant to several nursery friends, and upon hearing of her predicament, they kindly shared it back with her.

However, Nancy Goodwin yearned for a life free from such predicaments. She was no longer teaching music, and even with additional help in the nursery, she had less and less time for her garden. She longed for more time to spend creating the colorful displays for which she had become known. Of her two options, selling the nursery was not a solution because she wished to protect the highly regarded Montrose Nursery name. A more onerous possibility, closing, seemed to be the only suitable decision. It was most difficult for Nancy, but after ten years of building her fine nursery, she closed the door in 1993.

Since that time, Nancy has given her undivided attention to the garden at Montrose. Its fabulous displays have become legendary, and it is a mecca to gardeners and plant lovers alike. She gives scheduled tours four times each week and makes special appointments when asked. Garden visits conclude with a stop by Nancy's "shopping mall" where Montrose plants of cyclamen and 'Montrose Ruby' are for sale. A garden visitor will see not only a wonderful garden at Montrose, but may depart with a stunning souvenir plant bearing the name of Nancy Goodwin's remarkable creation.

Reference

Montrose Nursery Catalogue. Spring 1992

Acknowledgment

Nancy Goodwin

Photograph courtesy of Nancy Goodwin.

DAVID MOOBERRY

David Mooberry

Phlox paniculata 'David'

Arriving in Chadds Ford, Pennsylvania, on a sunny mid-July day in 1978, an observant horticulturist believed he was destined to select a certain parking place in front of a berm of wildflowers at the Brandywine River Museum. As he got out of his car, the driver noticed a large, white-flowered plant. On closer inspection, he discovered the plant was a pristine specimen of the native garden phlox entirely without the mildew disfiguring others around it. Excited about his discovery, he ran into the office and persuaded FM Mooberry, Coordinator of Horticulture at the Brandywine Conservancy/Brandywine River Museum, to accompany him to the parking lot for another look.

The driver happened to be Richard Simon of Bluemount Nurseries, Monkton, Maryland, no stranger to new plant discoveries. Mooberry was so pleased by Simon's discovery that she encouraged him to ensure the plant's survival. Without hesitation, he whipped out his shears and snipped five shoots of suitable cutting material, which he carefully stowed in a plastic bag. Simon took them to his propagation house where he rooted all five cuttings. Believing that the only way to keep a good plant is to give it away, Simon gave four of the five rooted cuttings to friends, one of whom was Dale Hendricks of North Creek Nursery in Landenberg, Pennsylvania. After observing the plant's performance, Hendricks wanted to make it available to gardeners.

For its introduction, the phlox discovery needed a name. Simon went back to Mooberry and asked her what to call it. Without hesitation, she declared it should be named for her husband, David, stating that this was "a good name for a big, bold plant." By giving his name to the fine phlox, she was saying thank you for his continued support of her work. Hendricks introduced *Phlox paniculata* 'David' in 1991.

Although FM's career has always dealt with plants, David is not a gardener. In 1954 his work with the DuPont corporation brought him to Delaware from Chicago, where he and FM continue to make their home. Today they are both retired and enjoying together their own constantly evolving garden, with hands-on by FM , and the nurturing support of David.

Phlox paniculata 'David' is a vigorous form of the native phlox. FM believes it possesses its strong characteristics because it was a natural selection from a native stand. Although it does not come true from seed, it is easily propagated from cuttings and is widely available in retail nurseries. With its relative mildew resistance and large pyramidal-shaped panicles of showy white tubular flowers, this perennial provides the gardener a fine selection of this native garden plant. It certainly impressed the leaders of the perennial plant industry. *Phlox* 'David' was selected the 2002 Perennial Plant of the Year by the Perennial Plant Association, its highest acclaim for a plant.

Thanks to FM, this handsome member of the summer garden well represents David Mooberry's strong supporting role in his wife's gardening endeavors. And, thanks to Richard Simon… for choosing the perfect parking place.

Acknowledgments
FM Mooberry
Richard Simon

Photograph by Pat Mooberry.

MT. AIRY ARBORETUM

Arboretum Center, Mt. Airy Forest, Cincinnati, Ohio

Fothergilla major 'Mt. Airy'

The stunning springtime show of this fothergilla attracted the attention of Michael Dirr when he visited the Mt. Airy Arboretum in Cincinnati, Ohio, on a May field trip from Ohio State University in the mid-1970s. A closer inspection of this eye-catching plant revealed its showy white flowers were actually exceptionally large, honey-scented round bundles of stamens. Later, an equally wonderful seasonal attribute was revealed in the plant's fall color: a dependable brilliant yellow, orange, red, and purple.

When Dirr revisited the plant in 1990, he described it as "somewhat mounded and distinctly suckering-stoloniferous" growing 5' tall and 6' wide. Believing it to be an exceptional form of *Fothergilla major*, Dirr shared his discovery with nurseries and christened it for the garden where it was found. His enthusiasm for 'Mt. Airy' has helped promote it to become an extremely popular garden shrub. This native plant is simple to cultivate and happily grows in sun or shade from Minnesota to Georgia.

Mt. Airy Arboretum is an outstanding garden of 120 acres located within Mt. Airy Forest, the largest of Cincinnati's parks. Before being acquired by the Cincinnati Park Board in 1911, the approximately 1,500 acres of land in Mt. Airy Forest had been used for farming and raising dairy cattle. At the time the city decided to purchase it, the tract had been rendered unproductive from overuse.

The city's original intent was to create a conventional recreational park, with open spaces of grass and traditional park equipment, but George E. Kessler, author of the 1907 Cincinnati park system plan, proposed that the land be reforested. In 1913 State Forester Edmund Secrest began replanting, and the first municipal reforestation project in America was created. Between 1913 and 1920, Secrest planted one million trees, a combination of hardwoods and conifers, and in 1929, made plans for the special area within the forest that was to become the arboretum.

Under the sponsorship of the Federated Garden Clubs of Cincinnati and Vicinity, planting for the arboretum began in 1932. In 1935 a division of the Civilian Conservation Corps was created to work at the forest. Through federal funding, additional planting and building took place in both the Arboretum and the park. Another milestone was the construction of the Arboretum Center in 1953. The building, which embodies the theories of Frank Lloyd Wright and was designed by prominent Cincinnati architect R. Carl Freund, serves as the office of the arboretum's horticulturist and provides a venue for instructional programs.

The Mt. Airy Arboretum is located in the northern corner of the Mt. Airy Forest. Its extensive collections of trees, flowers, and woody plants provide enjoyment and education for all visitors, especially the people of Cincinnati. Those who explore the area northwest of the Arboretum Center may, with luck, discover the parent of all 'Mt. Airy' fothergillas, the terrific plants which honor a fine horticultural institution.

References
    "A Guide to Art and Architecture in Cincinnati's Parks."
        Cincinnati: 1995.
    Dirr, Michael A. " 'Mt. Airy' Fothergilla Makes Its Own
        Beautiful Statement." *Nursery Manager* August 1991:
        52+.
    "Mt. Airy Arboretum Guide." Cincinnati Board of Park
        Commissioners
    http://www.nobleplants.com/introductions/fothergilla.html
    http://www.cince-parks.org/parks/text/mtairy,html

Acknowledgments
    Michael Dirr
    Paula Miller

Photograph by Michael Dirr.

JANE PLATT

Jane Platt

Magnolia stellata 'Rosea Jane Platt'

The childhood home of Jane Kerr Platt in Portland, Oregon, began as the residence of three young bachelors, one of whom became Jane's father. Twenty-six-year-old Peter Kerr arrived in Portland from Scotland in 1888, and went into the grain-exporting business. Two years later, he and his brother along with Peter's business partner purchased 13 acres with a small cottage that became a bachelor residence they called Cliff Cottage Club. The cliff-top land on the outskirts of Portland, with its spectacular setting on the bluffs along the west bank of the Willamette River, was known as Elk Rock, and it eventually became one of the finest gardens in the northwest United States.

The two other members of the Cliff Cottage Club married and left Peter to purchase the property for himself. When he married in 1905, he brought his wife, Laurie King, to live with him at the cottage. After the birth of two daughters, Anne and Jane, the Kerrs decided to build a larger home on the property. Peter wanted a manor house surrounded by natural landscape reminiscent of the Scottish homes he had known in his youth. He hired John Charles Olmstead from the Olmstead Brothers

Landscape Architecture firm of New York to site the home and design gardens that would blend into the natural beauty of the Oregon countryside and include a view of Mt. Hood.

The home was completed in 1916, but the gardens proved a much greater and more time-consuming challenge. Tons of rock were dynamited and the heavy clay soil was amended. Eventually the garden fulfilled Peter's dreams of meandering paths, spectacular views, and an array of glorious plants. According to Jane, "It (Elk Rock) was father's great love and recreation." Peter Kerr spent every free moment working in his garden until his death in 1957.

The daughters, Anne and Jane, inherited their father's estate and wanted to preserve it intact. In order to do this, they gave the house and gardens, now known as the Bishop's Close, to the Episcopal Bishop of Oregon. Their gift included an endowment for the garden's care and maintenance and stipulated it be open to visitors.

If environment plays a role in one's character, then it follows that Jane Kerr would become a marvelous gardener in her own right. Born February 14, 1908, Jane's early schooling was in Portland, but she was sent to Westover, a boarding school for girls in Connecticut, for her high school years. After Westover she went to France to study art. When she returned to Portland, her passion for gardening soon surfaced.

Another young Portland native had also returned home from world travels about the same time. He, too, was drawn to the land. In 1937, John Platt purchased two and a half acres of an old orchard with a small cottage in Portland's West Hills and wished to create a garden. Knowing about Peter Kerr's gardening accomplishments at Elk Rock, John sought gardening advice from Kerr's daughter, Jane. John and Jane's consultation on the making of a garden turned out to be one for life and they were married in 1939. John often claimed that Jane had married him for his property, and Jane admitted that could well be true, "what with the eighteen inches or more of the acid loam soil..."

The Platts began their garden immediately. During World War II, while John served in the Navy, Jane tilled a Victory Garden and cared for the first of their two sons, John, born in 1943. In 1945, when John returned from the War, garden construction began in earnest. However, when their second son, David, was born in 1948, family responsibilities became greater and consumed more time. John's career kept him increasingly busy and even though the couple continued to consult one another about their garden, in the early 1950's, John's time for gardening almost ceased to exist.

Without hesitation, Jane took over the garden's development. She found several gardeners and a landscape designer to help and by the early 1960's she had incorporated the entire two and a half acres into what she called her "painting". Reflecting her artistic training, Platt composed a garden of small spaces, each combining textures and color while maximizing the effects of light, especially in the autumn. Her eye for design and her knowledge of plants allowed her to combine thousands of species into a stunning presentation, although, like many gardeners, she was often faced with having to remove existing plants to make room for new ones. Perhaps her gardening philosophy helped; "Caring," she declared "is an essential part of gardening, but not sentimentality." In 1984, the Garden Club of America presented her with its Mrs. Oakleigh Thorne Medal "for the establishment of an exquisite garden incorporating rare and difficult botanic material into a design of incredible harmony, beauty, and distinction."

During the years Platt was developing her garden, she trained and inspired many young gardeners. One of these was an aspiring nurseryman, named Roger Gossler, who later became the manager of Gossler Farms Nursery in Springfield, Oregon. He first visited the Platt garden with his father, and for years afterward, continued to visit Jane and learn about the unusual plants she was growing. Gossler was one of the few people allowed to take cuttings unsupervised. The two exchanged and imported many plants and, in the 1970s, were responsible for introducing several from Holland, including the witch-hazels, *Hamamelis mollis* 'Pallida' and H. x *intermedia* 'Diane'.

Among the many plants in Jane's collection, Roger found an especially beautiful magnolia. He told Jane he wanted to propagate and introduce it, but the plant would need a name. The lady who was known for her shyness and retiring manner surprised him by saying, "Why not Jane Platt?" Gossler agreed to honor this marvelous gardener who was his friend and mentor.

Magnolia stellata 'Rosea Jane Platt' is a vigorous grower, performs well in a variety of soils, and exhibits a broad tolerance for heat and cold. The tree is rounded, shrub-like in form and typically no more than 15'-20' tall. The fragrant 3"-4" diameter pink flowers have 12 to 18 tepals, suggesting the appearance of a twinkling star. It is an early-bloomer which, because of staggered bud-opening, may remain in flower for as long as 20 days.

Gossler also noticed a petite 2' tall form of *Fothergilla gardenii* in Platt's garden. He introduced this small plant and also called it 'Jane Platt'. Except for its small size the shrub is like the species with white bottle-brush flowers and handsome yellow-red foliage in the fall.

Always willing to share her garden, Jane Platt gladly welcomed visitors, gardening groups, and professional growers. She was also generous with her plant collections and routinely shared seeds and cuttings. When John Platt retired in 1978, he returned to gardening with Jane. They spent a major portion of their time maintaining her creation, a labor of love that they continued until Jane died in 1989.

After tending and maintaining the garden for ten more years, John moved back into the original orchard cottage while their son, David, moved into the home his parents built. With the advice of friends like Roger Gossler, David took charge of thinning and pruning and maintaining his mother's garden. The originals of the plants named for Jane still grow there and specimens of *Magnolia stellata* 'Rosea Jane Platt' have been planted in the gardens at Elk Rock and the Catlin-Gabel School in Portland, Jane's elementary school alma mater. As wonderful legacies, her garden and the plants that bear her name continue to provide joy to many and memorialize her outstanding contribution to American horticulture.

References
Howard, Cathy. "A Close Encounter with the Truly Sublime." *Traditional Home* July 1992: 44-46.

McFarlane, Marilyn "A Scot's American Garden." *Garden Design*. Autumn 1987: 56-63

Platt, John W.S. "Oregon Eden." *House and Garden* February 1987: 143-144, 208+.

Verey, Rosemary, and Ellen Samuels. *The American Woman's Garden*. Boston: Little, Brown & Company, 1984.

Acknowledgments
David Platt

The office staff at Bishop's Close

Photograph courtesy of Cynthia Woodyard.

SAUL NURSERIES

Bobby Saul and Richard Saul

Dianthus plumarius 'ItSaul White'

Bobby and Richard Saul began their nursery in the early 1980's as a weekend business to produce landscape plants for the Atlanta area. Their small enterprise rapidly expanded into a multifaceted growing operation, and today consists of the nursery, a tissue culture lab, and a soil amendment company. The brothers' creative efforts have distinguished the Saul name, which is recognized for horticultural leadership.

Following graduation form the University of Georgia in 1977, Bobby Saul took his first job at the landscape firm of Billy Monroe in Atlanta. After several years, he decided it was time to begin his own landscape business. Meanwhile, Richard was working in north Georgia and growing ornamental plants in his spare time.

As gardening was becoming more popular during the 1970s, landscapers and gardeners were looking for new and different plants. Recognizing the changing commercial climate, the Saul brothers began producing perennials, starting with iris, daylilies, and hostas, then branching into an even wider range of plants, including shrubs and annuals. They quickly became a

149

major plant supplier to landscapers in the Atlanta area, and the colorful cutting-edge designs throughout the city could be traced to many of their selections.

On their primary growing site in the north Georgia mountains , Saul Nurseries built its first greenhouse in 1982. One of their earliest efforts was a seed mix of cottage pinks, *Dianthus plumarius*. The resulting seedlings varied widely in appearance and disease resistance. The following summer, all but one of the new seedlings perished from a fungus, but from these deaths, opportunity was born.

A white-flowered dianthus was the lone survivor. After propagating and observing this tough plant, they discovered it also possessed other worthy traits. It was an excellent evergreen groundcover, with blue winter foliage, and because of its later flowering time, was effective in extending the bloom season for pinks in the landscape. While these were admirable characteristics, its finest attribute was the obvious scent of vanilla. Leading with their noses, Richard and Bobby first listed the plant as *Dianthus plumarius* 'Vanilla', but in 1985, Richard introduced the clever "ItSaul" label and the dianthus became known as 'ItSaul White'.

The Sauls also use the label "ItSaul" for other aspects of their business. Their plug production company is named ItSaul Plants and their organic soil products are marketed under ItSaul Natural. However, the original nursery remains Saul Nurseries, and continues to be known for introducing outstanding plants. The list includes *Hemerocallis* 'Moontraveler', a repeat-blooming daylily resulting from a cross of 'Stella d'Oro' and 'Susie Wong' made by Richard in 1983. Though the name of the plant hints at the soft yellow color of the moon, it was actually suggested by a label found on a bottle rocket during a summertime celebration at the north Georgia nursery.

'Bewitched' is another dianthus introduction from the Saul brothers. They came up with the name as a playful derivative of its parent, 'Firewitch', an introduction from Sunny Border Nurseries. 'Bewitched' has reblooming light pink flowers with white centers encircled by a magenta ring and the silvery-green foliage of 'Firewitch. However, 'ItSaul White,' the first dianthus introduced by the Sauls, will always bring to mind this fine nursery and the innovative brothers from Georgia.

Acknowledgments
    Julie Evans
    Bobby Saul

Photograph of Bobby Saul by Linda Copeland. Photograph of Richard Saul by John Elsley.

SHADOW NURSERY

Emily Bruner, Don Shadow and Hoskins Shadow

Ilex vomitoria 'Shadow Female'

In the world of horticulture, the state of Tennessee is well-known for its large and active nursery industry. And no name is more inseparably linked with the industry than that of Don Shadow, the owner of Shadow Nursery in Winchester, a small town located in southeastern Tennessee.

Long before Don received his B.S. degree in horticulture from the University of Tennessee in 1963, it was a good possibility he would spend his life as a nurseryman. Don's father, Hoskins Shadow, grew up in his family's nursery, the Joe Shadow Nursery, in Winchester, as had his dad before him. The Shadow family had been in the business of growing fruit trees since 1872.

During the Great Depression, however, when the price of cotton in the southeast dropped to a nickel a pound, no one could pay for fruit trees. The Shadows sold a large number of dormant budded peach trees to an orchard in Ft. Valley, Georgia, but they could not collect. The bank foreclosed, and the Joe Shadow Nursery was forced out of business. For several years Hoskins worked throughout the United States in other nursery businesses, but in 1940, he once again became a nursery owner in Winchester, starting the Tennessee Valley Nursery where son Don learned about plants.

The Shadows have been responsible for introducing many fine plants, but one of the first "Shadow" plants was discovered instead by a frequent visitor to Hoskins Shadow's nursery. Fred Galle was a professor at the University of Tennessee in Knoxville and visited regularly. On one of those visits he noticed an unusually cold hardy yaupon holly, *Ilex vomitoria*, growing beside the nursery office. He asked about the plant's origin and Hoskins told him it had been a gift from Dick Jones, a Nashville nurseryman who had employed Hoskins Shadow during the 1930s. The specimen was not only hardy, it was also handsome, with its bright red translucent fruits set against large, dark green, almost rounded leaves. Galle named the holly *Ilex vomitoria* 'Shadow Female' for Hoskins Shadow and introduced it in 1952.

Another holly associated with the Shadows came to Don Shadow while he was still a student in Knoxville. During those years he met an outstanding gardener in town, Emily Bruner (called "Pinky" by her friends for her bright red hair), whose fine woody plant collection, featured a large cutleaf Japanese Maple and treasured *Davidia*.

Bruner was also well known as the teacher of weekly horticulture classes for fellow garden club members. During the popular segment "Ask Emily," she answered questions and shared her knowledge of plants, cuttings, seeds, and divisions. In 1993, as a tribute to their mentor, the Garden Club of Knoxville published, *Ask Emily about Gardening in East Tennessee*, a collection of horticultural notes from her classes.

Emily Bruner's knowledge of plants was well-known beyond her garden club circles. In 1960, as a favor to her friend James Swan, she supervised a landscape crew at his Swan Bakery, a Knoxville institution also noted for its fine landscape. While surveying the grounds, she discovered six unusual seedlings growing beneath a Chinese holly, *Ilex cornuta* 'Burfordii.' Puzzled

153

about their parentage, she found four large male lusterleaf hollies, *Ilex latifolia*, growing nearby. Convinced the seedlings were interspecific crosses between the Burford and lusterleaf, she planted them in her garden where they became handsome, pyramidal landscape shrubs: four males and two females. All had glossy, many-spined, dark green leaves, and the females produced large red fruits.

One day in 1963, Don was working at the university greenhouse when Bruner appeared carrying an armload of cuttings she wished to propagate. A severe hailstorm had damaged her prized hollies and she had pruned the broken branches. Shadow remembered being impressed by the form and fruit of the plants when he first saw them in her garden, and was glad to root her cuttings. Later he requested and obtained the rights to the plants and, in 1972, introduced the female as *Ilex* x 'Emily Bruner,' honoring the terrific gardener who discovered it. At Bruner's request, he introduced the male pollinator as *Ilex* x 'James Swan.'

The popularity of Emily Bruner's holly has extended far beyond Knoxville and serves as a fitting reminder of a keen plantswoman. Emily Bruner died in 1998 at the age of 97.

On October 1, 1977, Don Shadow began his own Shadow Nursery. Located near Winchester, the nursery extends over many separate tracts of land, allowing ample room for Shadow to grow his selections and discoveries in large numbers. By trialing his own efforts as well as the introductions of countless other breeders and explorers, he promotes and sells only the best. When Don lectures about the ornamental plant possibilities for the future, plant lovers dream about a long life and a pilgrimage to Winchester.

As passionate as Don Shadow is about plants, he can also entrance you with stories of his second love, exotic animals. Seriously committed to the protection of endangered animal species, he has set aside large tracts on his property for his collection. On a visit to the nursery, guests may encounter such exotics as French Poitou asses, an especially long-haired, big-eared donkey; the Damara zebra; and the Blesbok antelope. Visitors to the nursery always wonder what awaits around the next corner—another awesome plant, or another memorable animal.

But it is as a plantsman and third-generation nurseryman that Don Shadow has gained his reputation. Constantly searching for new and useful cultivars, he is in touch with plantspeople around the world. Talk to Don today and he will quickly describe the uncommon yellow fruits of hollies and nandinas or allude to a beech tree with golden leaves. Tomorrow the stories will be different.

Don Shadow is at the top of the list of the truly great plantspeople alive today. He has served as president of the Southern Nursery Association and the International Plant Propagators Society Eastern Region and is a former member of the Board of Governors of the American Association of Nurseries. He has received numerous awards including the Balentine Award from the Board of Trustees of the Southeastern Flower Show for significant contributions to Southeastern horticulture, the Medal of Honor for Outstanding Contributions to Horticulture from The Garden Club of America, and the Silver Seal Award from the American Federation of Garden Clubs. His energy is boundless, and his ideas unlimited. As his friends and family often say, Don will never run out of anything to do.

Reference
Siler, Nancy J., ed. *Ask Emily about Gardening in East Tennessee*. Knoxville Garden Club, Inc., 1993.

Acknowledgments
Melinda McCoy
Don Shadow

Photograh of Emily Bruner courtesy of Julia Huster.
Photograph of Don Shadow and Hoskins Shadow courtesy of Jennifer Shadow Fondrich.

BETTY SHEFFIELD

Betty Sheffield

Camellia japonica 'Betty Sheffield'

At the American Camellia Society's headquarters in Fort Valley, Georgia, more than 2,500 species of Camellias are registered, including *Camellia japonica*, C. *sasanqua*, C. *reticulata*, plus the lesser known species and endless hybrids. This staggering list contains many plants named for people whose stories might fill volumes. However, of all the plants of this genus, only one, 'Betty Sheffield Supreme,' a sport of the original 'Betty Sheffield,' can boast that its flower appeared on a United States postage stamp.

The story begins with a camellia named 'Mrs. F. L. Gibson,' a white-flowered *Camellia japonica* with pink stripes introduced in 1936 by F. L. Gibson of Thomasville, Georgia. In the early 1940s, Mrs. Albert B. Sheffield (Betty) discovered an unusual flower on a seedling of that plant in her garden in Quitman, Georgia. Described in camellia nomenclature as "a medium to large semi-double to loose peony form, with a white flower, striped and blotched red and pink with slightly waved petals," it became the camellia known as 'Betty Sheffield,' and the origin of more than 20 named sports.

The daughter of immigrants from Hannover, Germany, Betty was born Elsbeth Pannkoke in Milwaukee, Wisconsin, April 17, 1881. In 1916, she took a life-changing vacation to Florida. Her route passed through the town of Quitman, Georgia, where, during her visit, she met her future husband, Albert Sheffield. He courted her even when she returned to Wisconsin, and one year later they married. Betty joined her new husband in Quitman and delighted in her new hometown. Later, she encouraged her brother and sister to also make their home in Quitman.

After Albert died in 1930, "Miss Betty" became the horticulturist for Quitman. She tended her own garden, a "camellia forest" of nearly 300 varieties which surrounded her home, but she dedicated most of her time to beautifying her adopted community. The medians of Quitman's main residential and business boulevards, North Court and Screven, provided ample space for planting and she adorned them with so many camellias that Quitman soon claimed to be "The Camellia City."

A spunky yet diminutive lady, Betty Sheffield was a bundle of energy undaunted by her size. Former Thomasville, Georgia, nurseryman, Paul Hjort, remembers Miss Betty driving down the streets of Quitman peering over the steering wheel of her one-and-one-half-ton truck, an uncommon undertaking for any woman at the time. Because Betty was a friend of Paul's father, Sam, the Hjorts frequently left their undelivered Quitman orders with her. Later she loaded her oversized truck and distributed them to Hjort's customers.

Sam Hjort was the owner of Thomasville Nurseries, Inc., famous for many years because of its rose trial gardens. When Betty made her camellia discovery, she asked him to propagate her new seedling. He did so and was delighted to introduce it in 1946, as 'Betty Sheffield.' The new plant rapidly grew in popularity and recognition. In the winter of 1955–56 Rosalyn Alday visited Thomasville Nurseries to purchase a "a nice specimen of 'Betty Sheffield'" and drove away with a heavily budded plant, almost in bloom. Three weeks later she called the nursery and asked the Hjorts to come and see the extraordinary flower on her 'Betty Sheffield' bush. One of the twigs on a lower limb had produced a camellia with a new color form consisting of white petals edged in deep pink. Mrs. Alday gave permission to the Hjorts to propagate this mutation, and after four years of grafting and testing at Thomasville Nurseries, the plant was ready to be registered in 1960.

Rosalyn Alday was well-known in the gardening community in Thomasville and many people felt the new camellia should bear her name. However, she strongly believed all sport camellias should carry the name of the variety from which they sprang. She insisted that her new camellia should include the name of its parent, 'Betty Sheffield,' and her discovery was registered as 'Betty Sheffield Supreme.'

The unique beauty of the 'Betty Sheffield Supreme' received much attention, but it claimed its place as a flower legend compliments of the U.S. Postal Service. During the seventies, the American Camellia Society campaigned for a camellia to appear on a postage stamp, selecting 'Betty Sheffield Supreme,' the enormously popular flower discovered in then-President Jimmy Carter's home state, as its candidate. The Citizens' Stamp Advisory Committee of the Postal Service decided the 'Betty Sheffield Supreme' camellia should be one of four flowers honored, including a rose, a lily, and a dahlia, each individually portrayed on one stamp of a block of four new first-class stamps. The First Day of Issue ceremony, attended by many dignitaries including Mrs. Rosalyn Carter, was held April 23, 1981, at Fort Valley, Georgia, the home of the American Camellia Society. Unfortunately, the one person missing from the festivities was Betty Sheffield. She had died August 13, 1976, at the age of 95.

In 1971, five years before her death, the leaders of Quitman honored Betty Sheffield and recognized her horticultural contributions to the town by creating a Camellia garden in the median strip in front of the county hospital. When the world-renowned Edward Marshall Boehm porcelain factory elected to make likenesses of camellias for their collection, it is no wonder they selected the 'Betty Sheffield Supreme' to be their first.

The little lady from Quitman who loved camellias surely had no idea of the fame that would come to the plants that bear her name.

References
American Camellia Catalogue. Savannah:1949-51.

Hjort, Sam C. "Betty Sheffield Supreme." American Camellia Society Yearbook, 1959: 81-82.

"Recent Introductions form Southern Georgia." American Camellia Yearbook 1964: 41.

Acknowledgments
Ellen Beard
Ann Brown
Dorothy Copeland
Blondine Cunningham
Don Esmeraldi
Paul Hjort
Betty Horton
Ann Walton
Bailey White

Photographh courtesy of Blondine Cunningham.

NELLIE R. STEVENS

Nellie R. Stevens

Ilex x 'Nellie R. Stevens'

It was a close call. According to Mrs. Van Lennep, the 'Nellie R. Stevens' holly almost had her "head chopped off" before she was ever known. Having become holly collectors, Vida Stockwell Van Lennep and her husband, Gustav (Gus), were avid gardeners and had planted their own holly orchard in St. Michael's, a picturesque town on Maryland's Eastern Shore. The Van Lenneps were well-known for their holly interest and in 1952, Vida made a report about their holly orchard at a plant meeting of the Talbot County (Maryland) Garden Club. Eunice Parsons Highley, a friend from the neighboring town of Oxford, was also at that meeting, and when she heard about the Van Lennep's interest, she immediately asked them to visit her at her home, Maplehurst, to look at three unidentified hollies she was preparing to remove to make way for adjacent magnolias. Vida and Gus accepted the invitation and drove to Oxford.

In the world of holly enthusiasts, the Van Lenneps were still neophytes, but they compared each of Highley's hollies with the hollies they knew and realized each was different and unlike the other. They took cuttings of the plants, one female and two males to show at the Holly Society of America's annual meeting. The holly experts at the gathering were also mystified by the cuttings. Full of new hope for the previously doomed hollies, the Van Lenneps returned to St. Michael's and propagated the cuttings. After evaluating the plants, Gus Van Lennep was most impressed with the female clone and named it 'Nellie R. Stevens' to honor the lady who originally planted the seeds of the now-famous holly in her garden at Maplehurst. He introduced it to the commercial trade in 1954.

Nellie Robinson Stevens was born in 1866 on a farm near Oxford. Her parents were Edward John Stevens and Mary Ann (Markland) Stevens. When Nellie was 14, the family built and moved to a charming waterfront house in town. She and her six siblings grew up in their beautiful home the family called Maplehurst, a name perhaps suggested by the grove of maples they planted on the property.

It is believed that Nellie Stevens graduated from the Baltimore Normal School where she acquired her passion for learning and her desire to teach. Literature, music, and art were her favorite studies, but she always had time for athletics, a more unusual pastime for females of her day.

According to letters now kept in the Oxford Museum, "Miss Nellie," as she was affectionately called, was a delightful, respected teacher, and later principal, at Oxford High School. Her unbridled enthusiasm for learning and abundant energy inspired her students who enjoyed her classes and eagerly participated in the many extracurricular activities she organized.

To the residents of Oxford, Nellie Stevens was a popular "mover and shaker" whose efforts provided them opportunities for enrichment and entertainment. One of her most successful was a citizen's reading club. Also at Nellie's suggestion, the Tent Chautauquas—traveling concerts, lectures, and recitals popular in the early 1900s—regularly stopped at Oxford.

It is no secret, either, about Nellie Stevens's passion for gardening. When former student and later teaching colleague Erma B. Stewart was asked in 1956 to write a tribute to "Miss Nellie," she penned the following as part of her memories: "She interested pupils in beautifying the town by planting flowers and shrubs in their school yards and at home. She usually had flowers, either cut ones or those in pots, on her desk." In addition to her community gardening efforts, Nellie planted and tended her beautiful garden at Maplehurst

The passionate gardener was also an adventuresome traveler who never passed an opportunity for collecting new plants and trying them in her Maplehurst garden. According to one tale, a large boxwood came from a cutting Nellie took on a visit to Williamsburg. And it was on a trip to the United States Botanic Garden in Wahsington, D.C., around 1900 that she collected the seeds destined to become her namesake holly.

Neither Nellie nor her sister Ida Virginia ever married. They continued to live a genteel life at their family home and became the mistresses of Maplehurst after their mother's death in 1914. Nellie predeceased Ida in 1942, and Ida remained at Maplehurst until her death in 1951. Maplehurst then became the home of their niece Eunice Highley who took an immediate interest in the garden. Fortunately for gardeners everywhere, she contacted the Van Lenneps before renovating the garden.

After Van Lennep named the female holly for Nellie Stevens, Highley decided not to remove the hollies and to name the two males. One became 'Edward J. Stevens' for Nellie's father, and the other 'Maplehurst' for her garden. Highley gave cuttings to the National Arboretum in 1958. There are no records 'Maplehurst' was ever introduced commercially, but, 'Edward J. Stevens' was introduced by Van Lennep in 1958, and all three hollies were registered with the American Holly Society in 1967.

W. F. Kosar, a research horticulturist at the National Arboretum, determined Ilex aquifolium and Ilex cornuta were the parents of all three hollies. Both plants are listed in the 1900 collection of the U.S. Botanic Garden where Nellie found the seeds. In all three progeny, evidence of the Ilex cornuta parent can be seen in the leaves, which remain convex and are the same dark green color, yet they are less stiff and have shorter spines.

The leaf margins of 'Nellie Stevens' bear two to three spines, and the leaf veins are conspicuously depressed on the upper surface. 'Edward J. Stevens' possesses one less spine on the margins, and the leaf veins are less depressed. 'Maplehurst' is the smallest of the three shrubs and has a slightly narrower leaf with margins noticeably curled under with one to two spines, and a tip spine pointing downward at 90 degrees. All three evergreen shrubs are vigorous growers and become 18' to 25' tall with a horizontal branching habit. 'Edward' and 'Maplehurst' are mostly conical in form, 'Nellie' more columnar. 'Nellie' produces showy orange-red berries without the absolute need of a male clone, a significant benefit to gardeners. With her impressive attributes, the Nellie Stevens holly has become hugely popular throughout the Southeast and in the mid-Atlantic states. 'Edward J. Stevens' is useful to gardeners as a companion-pollinator for female hollies.

In a fitting tribute to Nellie Stevens and her famous namesake, the site for the 100th anniversary celebration of the American Holly Society in 2000 was Maplehurst, now the home of Jennifer and Edmund Stanley, Jr. The year 2000 also marked the centennial birthday of the planting of the seeds of the original 'Nellie R. Stevens' holly. Thanks to the serendipitous timing of the Talbot County Garden Club meeting and the subsequent Highley–Van Lennep discussion, 'Nellie R. Stevens' remains a permanent resident at Maplehurst. And wherever she grows, the holly provides a wonderful reminder of a remarkable lady.

References

Dirr, Michael A. *Manual of Woody Landscape Plants.*
    5th edition. Champaign: Stipes Publishing LLC, 1998.
Eisenbeiss, Gene K. "Field Notes." *American Nurseryman* Dec.
    15, 1985: 106.

Acknowledgments

Marcie Hawkinson
Vida S. Van Lennep

Ann McIntire
Sarah McNault
John Ruter
Virginia Sappington
Jennifer and Edmund A. Stanley, Jr.
Talbot County Historical Society

Photograph courtesy of Jennifer Stanley.

HELENE STRYBING

Helene Strybing

Leptospermum scoparium 'Helene Strybing'

The Strybing Arboretum in San Francisco's Golden Gate Park is a magnificent setting enjoyed by thousands of people each year. That it even exists is mainly due to the generosity of Helene Strybing. The idea for an arboretum originated during the park's early days in the 1870's, but Strybing provided the means to make it a reality.

On her death in 1926, at the age of 81, she bequeathed funds to the city of San Francisco for "the laying out, arrangement, establishment and completion of an Arboretum and Botanical Gardens to be situated in Golden Gate Park…." It was "to contain especially a collection of trees, shrubs and plants indigenous to, or characteristic, of California." In addition, "plants used for medical purposes, whether native to California or not, shall be given special consideration in this collection."

Strybing's instructions also directed that all trees, shrubs, and plants be properly labeled and that the Board of Park Commissioners of the City and County of San Francisco operate and maintain the Arboretum and Botanical Gardens. She further requested a bronze memorial tablet to recognize her late husband, Christian M. Strybing, with an accompanying acknowledgment of their gift of the Arboretum and Botanical Gardens for the benefit of the city of San Francisco.

Little is known of the wealthy widow's life. Helene Jordon immigrated to the United States from Germany, where her father, Ernst Jordon, was pastor of a Lutheran church in Romstadt. She married Christian Strybing, a successful California businessman. After he died in the 1890's, Helene lived almost another 30 years.

Helene Strybing's motives for providing an arboretum for San Francisco are unknown, but the intentions for her estate were clearly designated in her will. After her immediate bequest to the city, she created a trust fund for her brother and sisters in Germany that provided monthly payments until their deaths. When her last sibling died in 1939, the remainder of her estate, approximately two hundred thousand dollars, was given to the Board of Park Commissioners.

Actual construction work on the arboretum began in 1937 under the leadership of Eric Walther, who served as the first Director from 1937 until he retired in 1957. During Walther's tenure, the Strybing Arboretum's accomplishments were highly acclaimed. Always mindful of the benefactor's stated mission of meeting the needs of the community, Walther significantly increased the size of the plant collection and used it as the core of his educational programs.

Eric Walther began working at Golden Gate Park in 1918, long before he become Director. When he arrived at the gardens he discovered a collection of leptospermums. The plants had been planted around the New Zealand building at the Panama Pacific International Exposition of 1915 and were inherited by the park afterwards. Leptospermums, natives of New Zealand, Australia, and other southwest Asian countries, are known as tea trees, or by the New Zealand Maori name, manukas. They grow into shrubs and small trees with aromatic foliage, some-times used for medicinal teas. A profusion of small rose or white flowers cloak their branches in the spring. Walther became enamored with their beauty and imported additional ones from New Zealand to add to the gardens.

One of the new plants was *L. scoparium* 'Keatleyi'. In 1949 Walther collected seeds from this plant and sent them to the arboretum's nursery for germination. One seedling became a compact shrub, hardy in the San Francisco area, and produced large, cardinal red flowers with wavy-edged petals. The plant was so stunning in flower that Walther deemed it worthy of bearing the name of the arboretum's patron, and named it *Leptospermum* 'Helene Strybing'.

This splendid plant received the California Horticulture Society Award in 1966 and remains a favorite selection for California gardeners, especially in San Francisco where it flowers year-round. Moreover, its flower-covered branches are increasingly popular as cut flowers. Helene Strybing's vision created one of America's finest gardens and through the fine work of Eric Walther, we also have an excellent plant that bears her name.

References

Dawson, Marty. "A history of *Leptospermum scoparium* in cultivation: garden selections." *The New Plantsman* 1997: 67-68.

McClintock, Elizabeth. "The Strybing Arboretum and Botanical Garden of Golden Gate." *California Horticulture Journal* 1970: 60-65, 74.

Menzies, Arthur. "Plant Awards for 1966: *Leptospermum scoparium* 'Helene Strybing'." *Journal of the California Horticultural Society* 1967: 167.

Reiter, Victor, Jr. "*Leptospermum scoparium* 'Ruby Glow'." *Journal of the California Horticultural Society* 1963: 19-20.32.

Acknowledgments

Kathleen Fisher
Barbara Pitschel
RG Turner, Jr

Photograph courtesy of the collections of Strybing Arboretum Society, Helen Crocker Russell Library of Horticulture.

SUNNY BORDER NURSERIES

Robert Bennerup

Veronica 'Sunny Border Blue'

Robert Bennerup, founder of the well-known and respected American nursery Sunny Border Nurseries, is responsible for developing its most famous plant, which has a decidedly international pedigree. Born in Denmark on April 1, 1903, Bennerup came to the United States in 1924 to escape the aftermath of World War I. The young Dane was eager to leave behind a devastated Europe and to find a new life in America.

Trained in horticulture at the Vilvade Trade School near Copenhagen, Bennerup found work as a gardener at various estates of wealthy New Englanders. At one of these estates he met his future wife, Claudia Audet, a young woman from a rural French Canadian family who was being trained as a governess and cook. Neither Robert nor Claudia spoke the other's language, but they fell in love and were married on September 29, 1929.

After their marriage, Robert Bennerup began his own landscaping installation business in Tuckahoe, New York, and worked on many large properties throughout the region, including sites in New York, Connecticut, and New Jersey. One of the landscape architects who often hired him was Beatrix Farrand. Perennials were important in her design work, and she depended on Bennerup's ability to provide the plants. Few sources of perennials were available in those years and he was often unable to locate her selections, or those of other designers. Bennerup quickly realized the opportunity and decided to start his own perennial plant nursery, laying the foundation for what eventually became his main career.

Winter was a quiet time for landscape installers in New England, and Bennerup watched many of his wealthy clientele retreat to Florida. Astutely, he found another opportunity in their exodus: He drove to Palm Beach and offered his services as a floral designer to his clients at their winter homes. Raised in Europe where flowers were a habit, he was no stranger to indoor arrangements and was easily successful at his off-season occupation.

By the mid-1930's, during the years of dividing their time between New England summers and Florida winters, Robert and Claudia's family grew to include a daughter, Lillian, and a son, Pierre. Wishing to settle his family in New England year round, Bennerup purchased five acres of land in Connecticut and built their home. There he also continued his small perennial nursery, calling it Norwalk Perennial Gardens. In addition to growing bare-root perennials, some small conifers, and woody ornamentals, he opened a small retail outlet. The family remained at the Norwalk location until the fall of 1945, when they moved to Kensington, Connecticut, the nursery's present location. At that time Bennerup changed the name of his business to Sunny Border Nurseries.

In 1947, Bennerup learned his mother was ill and returned to visit her in Denmark. While in his native country, he explored developments in horticulture and compared plants being offered there with those available in the United States. Among his discoveries were two dark blue–flowered Veronicas, *Veronica spicata* and *Veronica subsessilis*. Bennerup immediately thought about hybridizing the two plants and took them back to his nursery.

The resulting hybrid was an exceptional veronica with round, dark green, crinkled leaves and persistent dark blue flowers. In 1949, with several dozen plants available, Bennerup added *Veronica* 'Sunny Border Blue' to his nursery catalogue. His introduction proved to be a popular and dependable plant that was easy to propagate by both divisions and cuttings. Its excellent garden value was recognized when it was selected as Perennial Plant of the Year in 1993.

Robert Bennerup died an untimely death in 1967, leaving the business to his wife, Claudia. Under Robert's leadership, the nursery had grown significantly, and without him, Claudia needed additional help to continue. She called upon their son, Pierre, who was working as a wine importer on Long Island. As a child, Pierre had helped in the nursery, but he never intended to become part of the business. At first he assisted his mother on weekends only, but soon he found the business challenging and enjoyable and, in 1969, purchased Sunny Border Nurseries from Claudia.

Pierre sold the nursery's woody plant division, closed the retail outlet, and converted the business to a container-grown perennial plant operation. Today Sunny Border specializes in producing plants of exceptional quality for retailers in the northeast corridor. An important focus is the introduction of new plants, and each year new flora from around the globe appear under the label, Sunny Border Gold.

Pierre was a co-founder of the Perennial Plant Association in 1986 and was its first elected president until 1988. He served on its Board of Directors until 1990. Other plant organizations have also benefited from his leadership. He founded the Connecticut Chapter of the Hardy Plant Society and served as president of the Connecticut Horticultural Society. In 2000, the American Horticultural Society presented Pierre with its Commercial Award, recognizing his achievements in the nursery business.

The love for flowers and gardens that led Robert Bennerup to establish Sunny Border Nurseries was inherited by Pierre, who continues to take the business to greater heights. Everyone who grows *Veronica* 'Sunny Border Blue' is growing a piece of a premier American nursery, the accomplishment of a family fervent about producing the very best garden perennials.

References
Sunny Border Nursery Catalogue 1997.
http://www.sunnybordergold.com/html/badge.html

Acknowledgments
Pierre Bennerup
David Culp

Photograph courtesy of Pierre Bennerup.

GEORGE L. TABER, SR.

George L. Taber Jr., George L. Taber, Sr.

Rhododendron 'George L. Taber'

One of the most popular of all southern garden plants must surely be the George L. Taber azalea. Widely grown in the region, it is perhaps the most cold hardy of the southern azaleas. With its particularly lovely orchid-pink flowers, it is one of the most beautiful, and its resemblance to an orchid provides its nickname, "The Orchid Azalea." Its cultivar name, however, commemorates the man who discovered it, the founder of one of the South's oldest remaining nurseries.

George Lindley Taber, Jr., noticed a sport on a lavender Omurasaki azalea one spring while admiring the flowers in the azalea garden at his nursery in Glen Saint Mary, Florida. Taber's records do not show the year he found this special flower, but his wife, Emily, remembers that when she and George, Jr., were married in 1935, the nursery was testing this azalea for introduction. She believes that her husband first saw the flower in the spring of 1928, the year before his father died. In 1938, when Glen Saint Mary Nurseries was convinced it had a prize azalea, it introduced the Taber azalea in its catalogue. George Taber, Jr., named it in honor of his late father, the founder of Glen Saint Mary Nurseries.

George Lindley Taber, Sr., was born in October 1854 in Vasselboro, Maine. His early education took place at the Moses Brown Friends School in Providence, Rhode Island. To seek his fortune, which would later allow him to start a nursery, he moved to Chicago and began his career with the Chicago Board of Trade. However, at age 27, Taber was diagnosed as having a weakened heart, a condition that prompted his doctor to prescribe a move to the South. For a born-and-bred Northerner, this was a substantial life change.

In 1881, Taber moved to north Florida near the small town of Glen Saint Mary, probably a spa at that time, where he purchased land along the historic Old Spanish Trail beside the Little Saint Mary's River. At last he could have a garden, and with a partner, Thomas Beath, he began to farm. They successfully grew potatoes and raised cattle, and were soon known locally as "Beef and Tater."

Building on their business, Taber broadened into fruit production. The first fruit crop of peaches was profitable, so the nursery expanded further into citrus and ornamentals. As Glen Saint Mary Nurseries prospered, so did Taber's health. He was a tall, large, and handsome man with a hearty laugh that was often heard throughout the nursery.

In 1906, Harold Hume joined the staff. A nationally known horticulturist and botanist, Hume authored many writings about citrus, camellias, hollies, and gardening in the South. His presence at the nursery significantly escalated the horticultural leadership of the company.

The following year Taber bought a large tract of land in Winter Haven, Florida, and the nursery increased its production of citrus. It was in citrus that the company first obtained recognition. In 1888, Taber had made arrangements to grow the Owari Satsuma, and in 1912, he acquired the rights to propagate and sell a late-maturing orange, developed by Mr. Lue Gin Gong. To complement that acquisition, the nursery also introduced the Hamlin Orange, an early-ripening variety. In 1924, Glen Saint Mary acquired Buckeye Nursery of Tampa, Florida, and, as a result, obtained the popular Temple Orange that

Buckeye had introduced. Because of "Glen's" leadership position in the citrus industry, the nursery helped standardize orange varieties and provided trees for growers in Florida and Texas. After World War II there was an upsurge in the planting of citrus groves, but by the early 1970s, the need for citrus trees decreased and Glen Saint Mary closed that part of its business.

Concurrent with the successful citrus business, the nursery also provided many ornamental plants for gardeners and landscapers in the Southeast. According to Emily Taber, Glen Saint Mary Nurseries was responsible in large part for introducing the people of north Florida to azaleas, dogwood, hollies, and camellias. She recalls when she first married George, Jr., and moved into the home built by her father-in-law at the nursery in 1882, she spent much of her time in the beautiful demonstration garden. The garden was open to the public and intended to encourage the use of ornamentals. Unfortunately, in the 1940s, a severe hurricane demolished the garden and it was never restored.

The popular southern azalea *Rhododendron* 'George L. Taber' honors a man whose personality, business training, and knowledge of horticulture built a small nursery into an acclaimed institution in both the citrus and ornamental arenas. Those who knew George, Sr., remember him with great respect. He was fair and honest in all he accomplished, and he engendered great loyalty from friends and employees. Taber's values are reflected in the nursery he created and its slogan, "Glen grown means well grown," indicates the importance the company gives to customer satisfaction.

The sense of family pride in the longstanding traditions are evident when one visits the nursery, now under the leadership of its current president, George L. Taber III. George L. Taber IV also works at the nursery, and George V is in kindergarten planting beans in paper cups and providing hope that the nursery which brought us the wonderful Taber azalea will continue for many years.

References

"A Short History of Glen Saint Mary Nurseries Company."
   1960.
Glen Saint Mary Nurseries Company Catalogue. 1938.

Acknowledgments

O. O. McCollum
Emily Taber
Magi Taber

Photographs courtesy of Magi Taber.

CLAUDIA WANNAMAKER

Claudia Wannamaker

Magnolia grandiflora 'Claudia Wannamaker'

If but one plant were to be chosen to symbolize the South, it might well be *Magnolia grandiflora*, the southern magnolia. The large, creamy white flowers with their distinctively sweet fragrance are often used to portray the romantic vision of a polite and genteel southern tradition. The magnolia named for a lovely southern lady, Claudia Wannamaker, could easily be the magnolia cultivar best suited to be this southern symbol.

Mary Claudia Harvin was born in Clarendon County, South Carolina, June 21, 1908, and grew up in Orangeburg. Her family moved there when she was four years old and she lived in the same town until her death in 1992. Claudia was a beautiful woman, and shortly after she graduated from Orangeburg High School, she became Miss South Carolina. An article in the *Orangeburg Times and Democrat* described her as "tall and slender, with light brown hair and hazel eyes," and reported that she was one of 15 finalists in the 1927 Miss America pageant in Atlantic

City. The next year Claudia married Alexander James Matheson Wannamaker (A. J.) of Orangeburg.

Claudia and A.J.'s daughter, Claudia Covington, recalls moving to the outskirts of Orangeburg in 1945 after her father returned from serving overseas in World War II. The Wannamakers called their new home "Attadale," the name of A.J.'s ancestral home in Scotland. On four acres of their new property, they decided to make a landscaped garden and hired Andrew Dibble, a local landscape architect, to provide the design.

The garden included a rose garden, a native garden, a vegetable plot, and additional plantings of southern species, such as camellias, azaleas, and magnolias. Many of the plants growing there were collected by Claudia as she traveled with her husband throughout the United States. Claudia's granddaughter, Dia Steiger, has fond memories of being led through the gardens of Attadale by her grandmother. She recalls the saguaro cactus and other exotic plants capturing her childhood imagination and the additional excitement she discovered beyond the cultivated garden walls where Claudia's peacocks, swans, and Shetland ponies resided.

Claudia Wannamaker was most at home in her garden and was often found there in her gardening costume of proper skirts and tall rubber boots. A patient gardener, she found great joy in planting young trees and watching them mature. One such tree was a Southern magnolia she received from a mail order nursery in 1945. When it arrived it was only 18" tall, but without a second thought, she planted the twig to see it grow. As it matured, she admired its appearance more and more, and several years later exhibited a branch at a local flower show. There the attractive specimen with its brown-backed leaves caught the attention of nurseryman John F. Brailsford, Sr., the founder of Shady Grove Plantation & Nursery in Orangeburg. Claudia enthusiastically pointed out that the comparatively small leaves and fruits, and relatively small flowers made cuttings from her tree especially useful for flower arranging. When she took Brailsford to see the tree, he was even more impressed and described it as "the most charming *M. grandiflora*" he had ever seen.

Brailsford believed people were entitled to better than seedling magnolias and wanted to make Claudia's tree available. Rooting southern magnolias from cuttings was not common place nor easy, and he experimented with this plant. His original attempts to propagate by grafting and air layering were unsuccessful. When his friend, Karl Johnson, Sr. of Bloomingdale Nursery in Bloomingdale, Georgia, gave him some tips, he was soon able to root cuttings from Claudia's magnolia. However, disaster struck when the main greenhouse burned and he almost lost his entire crop. Not to be deterred, he stuck several thousand more cuttings and in 1956 finally had sufficient numbers to introduce *Magnolia grandiflora* 'Claudia Wannamaker', the first cutting-grown cultivar in the trade, and, Brailsford claims, still the finest magnolia available.

Today all Shady Grove magnolias are produced using the nursery's own rooted cuttings. Four distinctive southern magnolias are among its offerings, each selected by Brailsford, and named according to its origin: Hasse, a nearby farm; Margaret Davis, the owner of a garden in Columbia; Smith Fogle, the long time superintendent of Shady Grove; and, Claudia Wannamaker, the lady who brought Shady Grove its most famous tree.

In addition to the leaf and fruit size, ' Claudia Wannamaker' has other desirable ornamental features. It produces flowers at an early age and at every terminal bud. At maturity, the tree becomes a broad pyramidal shape with horizontal branching to make it a good selection for areas with heavy snow and ice. In addition, landscapers find it to be reliable when it is transplanted.

The original magnolia still grows at Attadale. Claudia's daughter, Claudia Covington, hopes one day her mother's magnolia and the Attadale property will be included as an expansion of the park system in the city of Orangeburg. Meanwhile, Claudia's love of plants and gardening continues with her granddaughter. Dia is the Director of Wing Haven Gardens and Bird Sanctuary in Charlotte, North Carolina, and has appeared on the South Carolina Educational TV program, "Making Things Grow". Surely her grandmother would be proud.

References

Brailsford, John F., Sr "*Magnolia grandiflora* 'Claudia Wannamaker'." *Magnolia Journal of the Magnolia Society* Spring 1988: 6.

Shady Grove Plantation & Nursery, Inc. Price List 2000.

Acknowledgments

Janet Brailsford
John Brailsford, Jr.
Claudia Covington
Roberta Hagan
Carter Morris
Dia Steiger

Photograph courtesy of Claudia Covington.

WAVE HILL

Display garden at Wave Hill, New York City

Hydrangea macrophylla 'Wave Hill'

Aboard the parking lot shuttle to Wave Hill one of the passengers could be heard musing to himself, "I visit this place to restore my soul." Having discovered this tranquil oasis, New Yorkers are quick to show their affection for it. Wave Hill rests high upon the Palisades, the eastern cliffs along the Hudson River just north of Manhattan. Its magnificent natural vista across the mile-wide river to the towering western escarpment is a most welcome contrast to the concrete of everyday urban surroundings.

It is not surprising that everyone experiences renewal in this inspiring setting: families find a delightful destination for outings; landscape students seek to study its creative and colorful garden design; plant enthusiasts relish its artful displays of endless varieties. All of these reasons reflect Wave Hill's central mission of being "dedicated to exploring the interaction between human beings and the natural environment." The garden has been highly successful with its mission; its world wide recognition has brought visitors from across the globe to its gates in the Riverdale section of the Bronx.

The location of Wave Hill is the result of the growth and development of New York City. The first track of the Hudson River Railroad from Manhattan to the Riverdale Station was completed in 1849. Perhaps with the knowledge of the coming train access to the area, William Lewis and Mary Elizabeth Babcock Morris in 1836 purchased farmland north of Manhattan along the Hudson River. At "Yonkers Farm" in 1843 they completed construction of their Greek Revival style house and named it Wave Hill. Sadly, Mary Morris died after eight years and William left the farm soon thereafter to return to Manhattan. However, prior to selling the property two years later, the Morris heirs allowed a carriage road to be cut across the property, changing the setting of the house to a less isolated position and allowing greater access to Riverdale.

In 1866, William Henry Appleton purchased Wave Hill and owned it for the rest of the nineteenth century. He transformed the farmhouse into a Victorian villa and named it Holbrook Hall. At the same time he planted many of the copper beeches and European lindens remaining today. Appleton's friends were charmed by his home and many famous guests visited during the summers of 1870 and 1871, including the family of the future President Theodore Roosevelt, then a young teenager. When Appleton died in 1899, his friend Samuel Langhorne Clemens rented the home for the following three years.

As development of Manhattan proceeded northward, more roads were built and significant amounts of rock materials were needed. A convenient source for the stone and gravel was the Palisades, and before long quarries were destroying the magnificent cliffs. In 1900, in answer to public outcry, the Palisades Park Commission was created. The Chairman of the Commission was George W. Perkins, a citizen of Riverdale and active Palisades preservationist. Three years later, he purchased Wave Hill and two adjacent pieces of property. Perkins added new buildings and created gardens, the centerpiece being the pergola, still a prominent part of Wave Hill. When Perkins died in 1920, his widow, and Mrs. Edward Freeman, his daughter, continued to remodel the house and changed the name of the property back to Wave Hill.

With the opening of the Henry Hudson Bridge in 1937, easy access to Riverdale was accomplished and developers began to consume the land. To save Wave Hill, the Perkins and Freeman families donated the property to the City of New York. The city first called it Perkins Gardens, then, five years later, once again named it Wave Hill and began to develop the cultural institution we know today.

In 1968, Marco Polo Stufano became the director of the newly created horticulture department and transformed Wave Hill into a special garden. Features from the estate such as the pergola, greenhouses and formal garden areas were incorporated into his planting schemes. However, Stufano was an eclectic designer who made his own rules.

Wave Hill brims with innovative plant displays. The colors, the shapes, and the groupings of plants provide endless vignettes, some in more traditional flower bed arrangements and others in island gardens of meandering shapes. One example is illustrated by combinations of vivid tropical plants, metal hoops covered by twisting vines, and ribbed triangular aluminum sculptures only half visible among colorful leaves. In essence, Wave Hill is a plantlover's garden where the plants create interest. The resulting assemblage is a feast for the addicted and a treasure trove for the appreciative eye. Such a treasure was *Hydrangea macrophylla* 'Wave Hill.'

In 1986 Kenneth Burras, a guest from the Oxford (England) Botanical Garden, was touring Wave Hill when he stopped cold in his tracks. Burras, especially keen on variegated plants, saw a variegated lacecap hydrangea displaying unusual foliage. The white margins of the leaves changed to a yellow hue as they matured. Burras believed the plant was different from any other hydrangeas in the trade and suggested it be propagated. Stufano agreed and sent the plant to a nursery on the west coast for this purpose.

Soon after it appeared as *Hydrangea macrophylla* 'Wave Hill' in several nursery catalogues. An offspring of the original plant still grows at Wave Hill. With its striking green, white, and yellow foliage and its handsome pink and white lacecap flowers, this unusual, variegated plant is a perfect reminder of the extraordinary garden that produced it.

Wave Hill is a legend in its time, and other plants have been known to appear in the market place bearing its name. One example is *Alternanthera* 'Wave Hill', an eye-catching plant but one not introduced by the garden. Atlanta nurseryman, Bobby Saul, snipped a souvenir cutting, propagated it, and introduced it to the trade with the legendary name to honor its origin.

References

Feinberg, Jean E. Wave Hill Pictured. *Creation of a Garden*. New York: Harry N. Abrams, Inc., 1991.

Greer Gardens Catalogue. 1997.

Maxtone-Graham, Michael. "The Wizard of Wave Hill". *Sky Magazine* August, 1996:29-30,32.

Acknowledgments

Gene Griffith
Laurel Rimmer
Ted Stephens

Photograph by Linda Copeland.

FRANCES WILLIAMS

Frances Williams

Hosta sieboldiana 'Frances Williams'

A fleeting lapse of memory resulted in the naming of one of the most popular hostas ever grown, the classic plant, *Hosta sieboldiana* 'Frances Williams'. The serendipitous moment immortalized the name of a most deserving Massachusetts woman, Frances Ropes Williams. Long before hostas gained popularity in the United States, Williams recognized their value as the perfect plants for her own shady garden in Winchester, Massachusetts. With their wide range of color, form, size, and texture, hostas became her passion, and she began to collect, develop, and grow dozens of varieties. Along the way, she discovered the famous hosta that came to bear her name.

Frances' journey began in Salem, Massachusetts, home to the Ropes family since colonial times. She was born July 23, 1883, the eldest of Louisa King Farley and Willis Henry Ropes' three daughters. Her father was a successful businessman and enjoyed community activities, many focusing on gardening. He worked with children in Salem's public playgrounds, was a leader with the Boy Scouts organization, and was elected the first president of the Salem Garden Club. His boundless energy and longevity (he lived to be 91) were to be passed on to Frances.

Named Fanny Ropes at birth, she changed her name to Frances when she turned 21. Following her "can-do" independent nature, Ropes received a degree in landscape architecture in 1904 from the Massachusetts Institute of Technology and worked with the well-known Boston landscape architect, Warren H. Manning until 1906.

The Ropes family was known for their love of nature and outdoor activities and like her father before her, Frances was a member of the Appalachian Mountain Club. During a stay at the club's Three-Mile Island Camp on Lake Winnipesaukee in New Hampshire, she met Stillman Williams from Roxbury, Massachusetts. Their time together at the camp eventually led to the altar in November 1906, at which time Frances became a full-time wife. She and Stillman settled in Winchester, Massachusetts, and had four children: Constance, Robert, Stillman, Jr., and Louisa. Sadly and unexpectedly, Stillman died from pneumonia in 1925.

While the children were growing up, their mother made their home a popular gathering spot for their neighborhood friends: in their yard she had one of the first jungle gyms ever constructed. She also entertained children with delightful activities for learning and upon becoming "Granny" to seven grandchildren, she continued to design creative projects for them. Children adored this energetic and fun-loving woman.

Although Frances is best known for her contribution to the world of hostas, she was also a tireless community volunteer and played a key role in a number of organizations. The Herb Society of America was especially important to her. She served as its Corresponding Secretary and as its Curator of the Herbarium. In 1952, the HSA presented her its first Award of Merit for her "contribution to the present day knowledge of herbs." The New England Unit made her an honorary member in September 1966. It was not uncommon to find articles by Williams in the society's *The Herb Grower Magazine*. Her knowledge about a number of subjects and her creative talents provided many topics for her to share and her contributions made a significant impact on how herbs are used today.

In the early 1930's, when the children were grown, Frances became more involved with her garden. She collected plants from nurseries and friends, and began experimenting with hybridization of hostas. Her records included dated photographs of flowers and fruits and descriptions of her entire collection. A large part of her time was given to sharing plants and data with other hosta enthusiasts, taxonomists, and botanists throughout the globe, who, in turn, shared seeds, plants, and information with her.

Articles by Williams appeared in publications such as *Horticulture, The Journal of the New York Botanical Garden, the Brooklyn Botanic Garden's Plants and Gardens*, and, the Pennsylvania Horticultural Society's *Popular Gardening*. According to her grandchildren, stacks of old wooden orange crates filled with her papers, research, correspondence, and articles, lined two walls of her home office. After her death, many of these records were donated to the Andersen Horticultural Library at the University of Minnesota Landscape Arboretum.

The discovery of the 'Frances Williams' hosta occured in September 1936. Returning from her daughter's college in Poughkeepsie, New York, Frances visited Bristol Nurseries in Bristol, Connecticut. There she spotted, growing among a row of *Hosta sieboldiana* "one plant with a yellow edge" and presumed it to be a sport. Williams grew the plant in her garden for years, and when she was convinced her new hosta was unique, she gave a plant back to Bristol Nurseries. However, she also shared others with nurseries and friends, including Mrs. Thomas Nesmith of Fairmount Gardens in Lowell, Massachusetts.

One of Williams' many horticulture correspondents was George W. Robinson, Superintendent of the University Botanic Garden in Oxford, England. When Frances' daughter, Constance, visited Oxford in 1959, Robinson told her about his research with variegated foliage. Upon hearing this news, Frances wrote

Robinson about her yellow-edged hosta, called FRW 383, the name used by Williams in her system of acquisitions. She also asked Mrs. Nesmith to send him a plant.

Soon after he received the Williams hosta, the absent-minded botanist made Frances famous. During a lecture on variegated plants to the Royal Horticulture Society, Robinson was unable to remember the number on the new hosta's label. In that instant, he simply referred to the hosta as 'Frances Williams'. In February, 1963, he included the 'Frances Williams' name in an article for the *Journal of the Royal Horticultural Society*, thereby giving "valid publication" for the hosta. Almost certainly Frances's modesty never would have allowed her to use her own name, and without Robinson's lapse of memory, *Hosta sieboldiana* 'Frances Williams' would no doubt exist today under a less fitting designation.

'Frances Williams' may be the best known of Mrs. Williams' hostas, but this energetic woman hybridized and discovered numerous others. Ultimately she named two with special flower characteristics for a daughter and granddaughter. *H.* 'Louisa' was named for her younger daughter in 1969, and was one of the first variegated hostas to produce white flowers. Williams found the seedling in 1946 growing among *H. lancifolia* var. *albomarginata*.

A hosta with fragrant flowers resulted from a 1958 teaching experiment with her granddaughter, Susan. Granny taught Susan to take the pollen from *H. plantaginea*, a fragrant-flowered hosta, and place it in the flowers of *H. lancifolia* var. *albomarginata*. Several years later, when the young girl asked her grandmother, "Wouldn't it be neat to make some plantain lily perfume?", she learned that their hybridization experiment had borne fruit. A handsome hosta with fragrant flowers, only the third one in the world at that time, had been the delightful outcome. In 1966, Frances introduced the now popular fragrant hosta as 'Sweet Susan'. Instead of plantain lily perfume, Susan received a perfumed plantain lily bearing her name.

Williams named two other hostas for family members: 'Betsy King' for her great, great grandmother, and 'Carol', for

Susan's sister. She discovered 'Betsy King', a self-sown hybrid of *H. decorata* and *H. lancifolia*, in 1943. The plant is a neat and well-proportioned mound of dark green leaves with light to medium purple flowers and is considered to be one of her best introductions. *Hosta fortunei* 'Carol' resulted from a sport she found in 1967. Its heart-shaped green leaves are irregularly edged in white and splashed with gray-green and its flowers are lavender-blue.

The pioneering work in hostas accomplished by Frances R. Williams was a major stepping-stone to the founding of the American Hosta Society in 1968. In 1969, just before her death, the society presented her with a plaque to honor her for "devotion to the genus, for hybridizing, naming, and introducing many new varieties, and for inspiring others with a love for hostas." After she died on October 15, 1969, her daughter, Constance, with the help of Hosta Society members, created a hosta garden in the courtyard at the Massachusetts Institute of Technology as a memorial to one of the most unusual alumnae of this mecca of technology.

Further recognition of Williams' work occurred in 1986 when the American Hosta Society posthumously awarded her its Alex J. Summers Distinguished Merit Award. Constance accepted the honor for her mother and, as stipulated by the award, selected 'Frances Williams' to be designated the AHS Alex J. Summers Distinguished Merit Hosta for that year.

'Frances Williams' consistently appears on the "Hosta Popularity List" published by the American Hosta Society and remains one of the most widely grown hostas ever introduced. In remembering her grandmother, Susan Williams says, "Granny's handsome namesake is a fitting plant for such a wise and strong, yet gracious, lady."

References

Grenfell, Diana. *The Flowering Foliage Plant*. Portland: Timber Press, 1990.

Grenfell, Diana. *The Gardener's Guide to Growing Hostas*.
    Portland: Timber Press, 1996.
Schmid, W. G. *The Genus Hosta*. Portland: Timber Press, 1991.
Wister, Gertrude S. "Hosta 'Louisa'". *Bulletin of the American
    Hosta Society* March 1969.
Wister, Gertrude S. "Frances R. Williams and Her Hostas".
    Bulletin of the American Hosta Society March 1970.

Acknowledgments
    Toni Wright
    Steven Greene
    Susan Williams

Photograph courtesy of Susan Williams.

Index

192